NEW LIFE

Symbolic Meditations on the Promise of Easter and Spring

by Kathleen Wiley

Soulful Living, Inc.

Cover Photo: Kathleen Wiley at Seabrook Island, South Carolina
Cover Design and Illustrations: DARLENE
Copyediting: Carol Wiley
Interior Design and Publishing Assistance: DARLENE

Most scripture passages from the New English Bible (NEB),
with occasional use of the Revised Standard Version of the Bible (RSV).

Softcover ISBN: 978-0-9915661-3-6
Digital ISBN 978-0-9915661-2-9

1st Edition March 2014
2nd Edition February 2016

Published in the United States by:

Soulful Living, Inc.

DEDICATION

Dedicated to my friend Patty
for walking with me in New Life

TABLE OF CONTENTS

INTRODUCTION

**HE PROMISE** of Easter and spring is life after death, light after darkness, growth after dormancy, and movement after stillness. These pairs of opposite energies create wholes that are part of the life cycle. The cycle and its principles of growth are the same for all four worlds of the embodied reality of the self: physical, emotional, mental, and spiritual.

Easter and spring invite us to celebrate the new life that appears after winter's darkness. The church season of Lent is a time of preparation for going through the anguish, pain, hostility, and death that leads to resurrected life. Resurrected life is that which has been made new in us. Something that appeared dead now has an enlivened form.

The meditations in this book consider the symbolic truths of various scripture passages from *The Holy Bible*. Each of the meditations begins with a summary that connects the passage to the Easter story. We then reflect on the truth of the passage for our journey towards wholeness. There are forty meditations to accompany the forty days of Lent.

My writings are based on four fundamentals. First, the spiritual path of the West is Incarnation, not transcendence. We are called to fully embody God Within. Living in conscious relationship to God Within is our psychological and spiritual work. Second, as we are made in the image of God, our body mind reflects the Divine in us. All our thoughts, feelings, yearnings, emotions, sensations, and actions have a seed of God Within.

Third, the ego is who we think we are, the sum total of our conscious experiences. The Self is the totality of our psyche or soul. It includes our ego or conscious self plus all that is unknown about who we are. I refer to the Self as God Within as it is the psychic structure through which the Divine Mystery enters into our personal being. Clearing the pathway between our conscious self and God Within is the first step of our spiritual journey. This pathway has been called the ego-Self axis. When we are conscious of the flow of energy between our ego and God Within, we feel a sense of connection to the larger Mystery we embody.

Fourth, we experience God through the stirrings of the life force in our body mind. Everything that goes on inside of us has the energy of God Within. *The Holy Bible* is full of stories that illustrate the struggles we have as human beings. Relating to our life force, the energies of our body mind, as symbolized in the Bible, gives us a way to live more fully the truth of our psyche/soul. As we understand the metaphors, parables, and stories as symbolic representations of our inner workings, we reap a bounty of new life.

MY JOURNEY AND WRITINGS

I GREW UP in the Baptist church practicing the discipline of daily meditations. I would read a scripture passage and explore it using various commentaries, Bible dictionaries, and other study materials. I struggled to understand the meaning theologically and practically for my life. My journey led me to academic degrees in Christian Education and Counseling. I was drawn to train professionally as a psychoanalyst in the tradition of Carl Jung because I see his work as the best marriage of psychology and spirituality.

I write meditations on the scriptures with an eye towards what they mean about our psyche/soul. I consider the stories and images as symbols of our inner worlds, including our thoughts, feelings, sensations, intuitions, perceptions, impulses, and emotions. By contemplating the scriptures in this manner, we can access understanding of our selves as living beings who are manifestations of God. We begin to embrace and value who we are as everything in our nature holds a seed of the Divine.

Kathleen Wiley

Note about use of Self/self

IN JUNGIAN psychology, Self is the organizing principle of our psyche/soul and is the totality of our psyche. In contrast, the ego/self is an expression or extension of the Self. The ego/self is our conscious sense of self. It is what we think of as "I." Self, with a capital "S," is the larger whole of who we are. It holds all that is known and unknown in our nature. Jung once described Self as a part of God that God put in us so that we would know there is a God. In this book, you will see use of both self and Self to refer to these different parts. Because of the way I use these terms, I also use the spelling our selves, rather than the standard ourselves.

Notes About Use of this book

I have written the mediations in the tradition of devotionals to accompany daily Bible readings. I have followed The Revised Common Lectionary adapted for Episcopal use in the selection of passages. I have noted the entire scripture passage with each meditation while printing only selected verses of focus. I encourage you to read the entire passage from your Bible or one of the many available online translations.

The Glossary definitions are designed to be working applicable descriptions, not clinical or scholarly.

CHAPTER I

What Do You Seek?
Jeremiah 45:1–5

At Easter, we reflect on the prophecy of the temple being destroyed and rebuilt in three days. We know that this prophecy pointed to Jesus' bodily death and resurrection. The destroyed temple was the body. Our temple body is the sacred house of God and is the house where our ego, conscious sense of self, begins. Seeking to know God Within happens as we build, inhabit, and nourish our body mind.

Verse 5, "You seek great things for yourself. Leave off seeking them; for I will bring disaster upon all mankind, says the Lord, and I will let you live wherever you go, but you shall save your life and nothing more."

WHAT IS MOST important to you? What do you value more than anything else? So often, we become attached to things, ways of being, habit patterns, and conveniences of relationship to the detriment of our life and life force. C. G. Jung notes that neurosis occurs when the natural flow of our life force (libido) is thwarted. Instead of living in sync with our innate Self, we give up the felt knowing of our passions and take on imposed ideas, beliefs, commitments, and fleeting desires. We do what we think we should, or what is easy in the moment, instead of what we know our heart wants us to do!

Proverbs 20:27 says, "The spirit of man is the candle of the Lord, searching all the inward parts of the belly." Our inward parts, all the thoughts, emotions, feelings, sensations, intuitions, desires, and impulses are light thrown from the candle of God Within. Sometimes the light is dimmed or covered up by traits, behaviors, beliefs, or conditioned responses that have been learned. Our adaptive self can feel like who we are, even though it may mask God Within.

To live in sync with God Within we must differentiate between the learned or adaptive self and the innate, larger Self. We have to seek to see the root of our thoughts, feelings, pulses, and desires. We begin to do this as we see the roles we play (such as our profession, being a son or daughter, being the class clown, acting as a caregiver), our automatic feedback loops where a reflexive response is triggered by a particular affect or emotion, and the unseen, unintended communications that always seem to accompany our actions. By building a relationship to our self as more than any role, feedback loop, or unintended communication, we begin to differentiate parts of our self. We clear space for the voice of God Within to be heard We begin to recognize the differences between the learned, internalized voices and the voice of God Within.

As we gain consciousness and can distinguish between the voice of the learned and the voice of God Within, we can call on God Within for guidance, healing, comfort, etc. We open to awareness of the life giving impulses in all our feelings. We are able to do far more than our ego can do alone. We release activities, behaviors, relationships, projects, etc. that have become deadening.

Our psyche has a gradient or direction that our life force will follow. We do not have to force it. We only have to align with it. To do so, we must leave off seeking "great things for our selves" and "save our life." Our life, our life force, the flow of God Within is what matters! △

Inner Reflection

Take a few minutes to sit quietly and be aware of the life force as it pulses through your body. Connecting with your breath is one way to begin this awareness. Reflect on this time in your life and how your libido is moving. (1) What feelings, thoughts, actions, relationships, projects, etc. allow for the free flow of God Within? (2) Where does your life force get stopped? Consider holding the intention to "leave off seeking…and save (your) life." (3) What would you do differently beginning now?

---

(1) Relationship w/ children & grandchildren, siblings, close friends
Giving to charity & certain political entities
(2) When I choose to distract myself in unhealthy ways
(3) This –

CHAPTER 2

THE WISDOM VOICE:

James 3:13–4:12

Lent is traditionally a time of self-reflection and contemplation. We willingly give something up to make space for knowing God Within. As we seek to know our selves in relationship to God, we can hear the inner Wisdom voice. Wisdom leads us to an acceptance and integration of our true nature. We give up hiding from our selves. We find the ability to be straightforward and sincere.

Verse 17, "But the wisdom from above is in the first place pure; and then peace-loving, considerate, and open to reason; it is straightforward and sincere, rich in mercy and in the kindly deeds that are its fruit."

WE SOMETIMES struggle to distinguish between the voice of the Self (God Within), referred to as the Wisdom Voice, and the other "voices" that stream through us. Other voices include internalized statements of our parents, teachers, the media, and the church, as well as past desires and impulses we have now disowned. We have to face collective voices that ultimately go against life and differentiate them from the Wisdom voice.

In the story of Christ's temptation in the desert, Jesus faced the devilish collective voice that promotes gratification of every impulse, self-serving use of wisdom, and dominance over others. He stayed connected to what he knew to be his soul's truth and acted with Wisdom.

We find Wisdom through

connection to our larger Self or God Within. According to Kabbalistic teaching, Wisdom is the second emanation of God that flowed into soul at the time of Creation. Wisdom has been described as God's self-reflection. Alexander Cruden, in *A Complete Concordance*, states the following regarding Wisdom: "For that prudence and discretion, which enables man to perceive what is fit to be done, according to the circumstances of time, place, persons, manners, and end of doing." (page 559) Wisdom gives foresight and discretion. We call this insight—seeing into a situation, behavior, etc. in a new and deeper way.

The writer of James offers a description of wisdom that is helpful in knowing the voice of our Inner Divine nature. Wisdom is "in the first place pure." It possesses the purity of the universal life force that expresses itself in the soul or the Self. Throughout the ages, wise men have said, "Know thyself," and "To thine own self be true." Living from a place of wisdom means living out of the truth of who we are. It means being authentic, not trying to be someone we are not.

The other descriptors of Wisdom noted by the writer of James are inherently present when we live from the Wisdom of the Divine life force in us. We are "peace-loving, considerate, and open to reason"; we are "straightforward and sincere, rich in mercy and in the kindly deeds that are its fruit." When we live from the purity of who we are as a child of God, we can let others be who they are. By being who we are, we accept and are considerate of who others are. We do not have a need to make others into who or what we want. We are able to see together, to reason when there are differences, instead of creating conflict. These qualities manifest in our inner world also. We are accepting of all of who we are, as we practice consideration, reason, and mercy towards our selves.

Wisdom leads us to an acceptance and integration of the varied desires, impulses, sensations, thoughts, and feelings we have. The result is the ability to be straightforward and sincere. We give up hiding from our selves. We express an attitude that is "rich in mercy and in kindly deeds" as we interact with our selves and others.

Inner Reflection

Take a few minutes to reflect on where and when you have known the Wisdom of God Within. What were the feeling qualities of the experience? Where are you struggling now to hear Wisdom? Ask to know the purity of your soul in your impulses, desires, thoughts, feelings, etc. Look for the qualities of Wisdom noted in today's scripture as a guide to knowing the Voice of God Within.

CHAPTER 3

A NEW INNER MORALITY:
Jeremiah 7:1–15

At the time of Christ's crucifixion, the temple veil that kept people from the innermost Holy of Holies was torn open. Symbolically, the opening suggests a way of relating within our selves where nothing is hidden. All is seen. Mending our ways and our doings with our self is the first step in transformation. When we want something different in the outer world (relationships, environment, etc.), we must first change within our self.

Verse 5, "Mend your ways and your doings, deal fairly with one another, do not oppress the alien, the orphan, and the widow, shed no innocent blood in this place, do not run after other gods to your own ruin."

AS I WAS READING this scripture, it occurred to me that the instruction is one that we all need to adopt in relationship to our self. We easily see what these statements mean in relationship to other people. We forget that we also need a loving relationship to all aspects of our selves.

The alien, the orphan, and the widow represent energies in our psyche/soul that are cut off, abandoned, and isolated from our conscious self. These energies show up in thoughts, feelings, emotions, sensations, desires, perceptions, etc. that hold some bit of unconscious self that wants to be seen, acknowledged, and realized. We may feel threatened by them, so we pretend they aren't there.

The alienated aspects of our self most often evoke a sense of "Where did that come from? That's not like me." Undesirable, shame-invoking thoughts, emotions, moods, etc. often prompt the statement, "I do not feel like myself." "The devil made me do it." Something alien, or other than ego, is emerging from psyche. This something wants a place of appropriate expression in our lives. We often deny emotions, thoughts, and desires when they challenge our self-image or our stated values. Our defined idea of who we are and how we act may keep us from seeing other aspects of our self. Yet, the alienated emotions and desires are an expression of God Within too.

The orphaned aspects of our psyche are bits of our self that we once knew, but we did not tend. We had some awareness of the desire, yearning, or talent, but we let it slip into the background and go unconscious. Think about the dreams you had as a child, ages 8–12. What could you do alone for hours on end and be satisfied? Those dreams/activities hold the seeds of your life's work. Orphaned aspects of our self usually excite our gut and ignite our imagination when they appear.

The widowed aspects of our self start to grow and have a place in our sense of self, but then we set our conscious tending and dialoguing with them aside. We leave them behind as something else uses our energies, attention, and focus. The something else may be an outer world demand, an internal state of feeling, another desire, etc. Often the widowed energies make themselves known in our regrets. We realize that we cut off or lost connection to some piece of self that is valuable.

The alienated, orphaned, and widowed aspects of our self are waiting to be noticed, heard, and received compassionately. In any moment, we can choose to consciously connect with the energies caught in our memories, regrets, unbidden emotions, body experiences, etc. When we do receive these aspects, we mend our ways and doings with our self.

Mending our ways and our doings with our self is the first step in transformation. When we want something different in the outer world (relationships, environment, etc.), we must first change within. We encounter alien, orphaned, and widowed qualities in other people and situations as an invitation to know and integrate those qualities within our self. As we change our relationship to our self, our relationship to others changes.

Inner Reflection

Take a few minutes to reflect on the alienated, orphaned, and widowed aspects of your psyche/soul. What are your disowned feelings, desires, and talents? Where do you give up your heart's desires? How do you cut off parts of yourself? Invite those pieces of self back home to your body mind. Welcome them compassionately. Engage them in dialogue in your mind's eye and receive the gifts of energy they offer.

CHAPTER 4

A NEW ORDER:
2 Corinthians 5:14–18

The seasons of Lent and Easter invite us to reflect on the processes of change that include death and resurrection. As we join with the energies of the Self/God Within, something changes within us and ultimately around us. A new world emerges.

Verses 15-17, "His purpose in dying for all was that men, while still in life, should cease to live for themselves, and should live for him who for their sake died and was raised to life….When anyone is united to Christ, there is a new world; the old order has gone, and a new order has already begun."

IN JUNGIAN psychology, Christ is a symbol of the Self. The Self is the organizing principle of psyche (soul) that Jung described as "God Within us." The Self encompasses the whole of our psyche/soul, what is known and what is unknown. The self, with a small "s," refers to our conscious sense of who we are. The terms ego and self are sometimes used interchangeably.

Our ego or self is the psychic structure that mediates between our larger Self and the outside world. We need an ego to be healthy. Unfortunately, the phrase "should cease to live for themselves" has been misused to promote self-denial that destroys the bridge between our ego and God Within. As a result, our relationships to our selves, other people and the world around us suffer. We become an empty shell going through the motions of life. We lose connection to the vitality of our life force that comes from connection to our self. We may experience pockets of self-hatred, self-contempt, or self-destruction that handicap our ability to embody aspects of God Within. The result is that the self through which the Self flows is not strong enough to contain and channel the energies that want to take shape in the world.

We can also get caught in a limited and self-absorbed sense of who we are. Our ego/self may think and make choices as if it were the whole of our psyche/soul. We may act as if our momentary sense of who we are is all we are. We can have an arrogance and pride that forgets God Within. Perhaps, this is the state to which the phrase "should cease to live for themselves" is referring.

The Self sacrifices some of its wholeness and fullness each time it becomes limited by a particular form. The form may be an attitude, a belief, an emotion, a feeling, a passion, an intuition, or a behavior. The one attitude, belief, etc. expresses a ray of the whole psyche, but it is not the totality of God Within.. Our ego is a ray of the Self. It is an expression of the totality of our psyche or larger Self that is limited in time and space with a particular focus, purpose, set of experiences, etc. Each time we join with the energies of the God Within as they appear in the forms noted above, "there is a new world." Something changes within us and ultimately around us "as the old order has gone, and a new order has already begun."

The scripture reminds us that our ego must cease to live for itself and seek to live the truth of God Within. When we deny the momentary whims of our ego/self in order to live the desires of God Within, we are united with Christ. A new world order begins.

Inner Reflection

I invite you to consider the state of your ego in relationship to God Within. Where do you act as if your known, momentary sense of self is all you are? Where are you aware of the larger Self? How and where is God Within stirring? Ask God Within to show you the next step in being "united to Christ (the Self)" and experiencing the new order within your body mind and outer life.

CHAPTER 5

THE LIGHT OF DESIRE:
Psalm 13

Easter and spring usher in the physical reality of more light. The days become longer than the nights. When we experience a resurrection of our heart's desires, we have more inner light or consciousness. The warmth of our soul flows into our body and mind and grows new life in our world.

Verse 3b, "Give light to my eyes
lest I sleep the sleep of death."

Verse 6, "I will sing to the Lord,
who has granted all my desire."

WHAT IS IT THAT you truly desire? Look at your life and you will see! Your desires are mirrored in your body, mind, environment (the space around you), and relationships. Whatever the state, it reflects a feeling-toned state of consciousness that you hold in your psyche, knowingly or unknowingly. Take a moment to ask yourself the following.

Is your body the size and tone you think you want? Do your home and workspace reflect the beauty of your soul and soothe you, or is it cluttered and messy? Are your relationships supportive? Do your daily habits support your soul's desires?

Like the psalmist, we sometimes feel an absence of God when our body mind, environment, or relationships seem to create suffering and grief. We long for the peaceful feelings and balanced actions that oneness with God Within brings. As we seek to build a relationship to all the energies in us, we can follow the psalmist's example. He beseeches God, "Give light to my eyes lest I sleep the sleep of death." Psychologically, the sleep of death is to be unconscious—to be blind to what is within our nature, to be unaware of the totality of Self.

When unconscious, we are trapped in patterns of thought, feelings, and behaviors. We do not clearly and accurately see the internal states behind our automatic responses. We often blame an external God when we do not have what we want. Yet, the psalmist proclaims the Lord "has granted all my desire." Perhaps, the something that stands in the way of our desires is within us.

Our true heart's desires are not always the momentary long-ings or yearnings that appear. An immediate craving for a particular object may be an attempt to meet a need or want but may not be the true desire. A common example is reaching for food when we feel anxious or uncomfortable. What we really need is emotional comfort or nurturing, not physical food. Our unenlightened human nature often mistakenly reaches for a thing (food, consumer products, mood-altering chemicals, another person) when our heart's desire is for a particular feeling state (peace, assurance, confidence, well-being, and so forth).

Instead of "going to sleep," we can follow the psalmist's example and ask God Within to give us light—to help us see our soul's desire. We must be willing to see, without judgment or shame, what our impulses and yearnings are. By looking within to the nuances of our emotions, we become aware of what is bubbling inside of us. We can then act on behalf of our heart's desire, not the momentary or reflexive impulsive yearning.

Inner Reflection

Think of a problem area or question with which you are struggling. Ask God Within to help you see what desires are at play and what your heart's true longings are. Ask, listen, and receive that you may move from the sense of freedom that aligning with God Within brings.

CHAPTER 6

SAVED FROM SHAME:

Romans 10: 8-15

On the cross, one of the thieves being crucified along side Jesus recognized his Divinity. The thief acknowledged his wrong-doing and asked Jesus to remember him. Jesus said, "today you shall be with me in Paradise." We too can ask God Within to save us from the energetic death of paralysis that shame about our self brings.

Verses 11-12, "Scripture says, 'Everyone who has faith in him will be saved from shame'--everyone: there is no distinction between Jew and Greek, because the same Lord is Lord of all, and is rich enough for the need of all who invoke him."

WRITE ABOUT SHAME a lot because I have found it to be the number one bugaboo in people's psyches. It is often at the root of ego defenses that keep us from being real with our selves and others. Shame is a feeling that paralyzes; it thwarts our ability to experience fully, to think freely, to feel truthfully. We go numb, disown bits of our selves, and end up stuck. A false self takes the place of our real self. Sometimes, we end up not knowing what is real about our self!

The way out of shame is to move in sync with God Within. Psychologically, to have faith in Christ means to have faith in the Self, the totality of psyche/soul, that is the fullest expression of

God Within us. We have to risk believing "the power greater than" our ego that we experience as the still small voice of God Within. Somewhere in our body, there is a knowing of God Within even if we cannot consciously access it in a given moment. The Self holds all of who we are together even when we feel disjointed, scattered, or fragmented.

The image of a circle or mandala is a symbol of the Self. When we feel as if we're falling apart or flying into pieces, it can be helpful to draw a circle and fill it with colors, shapes, images, etc. that represent what we are experiencing internally. God Within can hold all the pieces of our self together even when the ego/self is not able to do so. A mandala or circle filled with self-representations helps us to remember this.

Moving towards wholeness consciously is a choice. We can hold onto ego/self defenses and never integrate bits of the self/ Self that show up in unpleasant and uncomfortable feelings, perceptions, movements, etc.; or, we can call on the larger Self for an attitude of compassion and a remembering of one's value (self-worth) that humanizes the shame (or other negative feelings) and makes it bearable.

When we reach for and practice compassion and mercy towards our inner experiences (feelings, emotions, fantasies) and our outer behaviors (words, actions, movements), something life giving happens. We are saved from deadening shame. Our energy flows. We are able to move more freely in the inner realm of our thoughts, feelings, perceptions, sensations, etc. The inner movement translates into new behaviors, attitudes, and ways of moving in our outer relationships (to self and others).

All parts of our ego/self (represented by Jew and Greek in the scripture) are acceptable to God Within. God Within is "rich enough for all". As we claim this truth, we are empowered to meet our thoughts, feelings, intuitions, and sensations instead of denying or dismissing them. △

Inner Reflection

Take a few moments to affirm to yourself that God Within is big enough to hold all bits of you. Be courageous and acknowledge the feelings, thoughts, impulses, fantasies, etc. that haunt you. Draw a circle and fill it in with colors and shapes that reflect the various bits of self/ego and God Within that you are experiencing in the moment. Breathe deeply and allow any shame to be humanized as you see the whole of who you are.

CHAPTER 7

THE GIFTS OF SEEING AND HEARING:
Colossians 1:9–14, Matthew 13:1–16

We live in a world of matter where we are easily seduced into thinking that what is concrete, literal, or fixed is the truth. Our minds become "gross"—filled with an occupation of that which is immediately obvious. The Easter story of crucifixion and resurrection remind us that reality is bigger than what appears in the rational, materialistic worldview.

Colossians 1:9, "We ask God that you may receive from him all wisdom and spiritual understanding for full insight into his will, so that your manner of life may be worthy of the Lord and entirely pleasing to him."

Matthew 13:15, "For this people's mind has become gross; their ears are dulled, and their eyes are closed. Otherwise, their eyes might see, their ears hear, and their mind understand, and then they might turn again, and I would heal them."

WISDOM AND SPIRITUAL understanding come from seeing and hearing beyond surface appearances and words. We live in a world of matter where we are easily seduced into thinking that what is concrete, literal, or fixed is the truth. We feel limited by our bodies and our environment, and we get stuck. We quit looking and listening because we assume there is nothing new to see or hear.. Our minds become "gross"— filled with an occupation of what is immediately obvious.

The idea that matter and the physical are only an illusion is an inviting, but deadly, alternative to the limitations of our bodies and environments. Many practices (including spiritual traditions) encourage us to dismiss our bodies and devalue the outer world. Techniques for leaving our body and transcending our felt experience are offered as ways to assert the power of the mind/ego over our felt experience.

When we identify with a "gross" mind or seek escape from our embodied, physical experience, we dismiss the reality of Incarnation. The Christian gospel affirms the reality of God becoming human and humans becoming god-like. Genesis states that we are made in the image of God; Jesus said to his disciples "ye shall become as gods." Spirit becomes matter and matter becomes spirit. We are called to embody Spirit, not to dissociate from our bodies and pretend to be Spirit.

The scripture from Colossians connects the receiving of "wisdom and spiritual understanding for full insight into (God's) will" to our "manner of life." Our life is the arena to which wisdom and spiritual understanding apply. Our daily activities, usual routines, customary interactions, or habitual ways are where we need to see and hear the instruction of God Within.

Our predictable ways of thinking, feeling, responding, or acting reflect patterns we have internalized intentionally or unintentionally, consciously or unconsciously. We stick with the way we are living without looking to see how God Within wants us to move in the moment. We think we know the truth of the situation, other person, or our self as "our ears are dulled, and our eyes closed."

Today's scriptures remind us that we need to seek wisdom and understanding in order to bring our daily manner of life in sync with the God Within.

We can find God Within in all areas of our lives, including our inner processes.

The work of becoming more conscious begins by seeing and hearing—knowing what is— within our body mind. Knowing our thoughts, beliefs, judgments, emotions, affects, perceptions, fantasies, sensations, and intuitions is the starting place for sharpening our abilities to hear and see. As we recognize the presence of God Within in all aspects of our lives, we can seek wisdom and understanding that takes us beyond the obvious surface appearances.

Inner Reflection

Take a few minutes to acknowledge where you feel "dull of hearing and sight." Where are you struggling to be free, to not be stuck, to have desired movement? Make a list of what you see and hear within yourself about being stuck. What do you know about it? What do you not know? Breathe deeply and direct your attention to the center of your body. Ask God Within for the needed wisdom and spiritual understanding to see and hear more fully and clearly. Watch and listen as you move throughout your day.

CHAPTER 8

DESTRUCTION FOR LIFE:
Isaiah 2:1–11

The celebration of Easter and the ancient rituals of spring remind us that life comes after death. The life force is freed when a form dies; new life comes. Learning how to use destructive impulses in service of life, instead of against life, is essential for our spiritual growth. Knowing what and when to destroy, and what and when to build is a gift of conscious relationship to God Within.

Verse 4, "They shall beat their swords into plowshares and their spears into pruning hooks; nation shall not lift sword against nation nor ever again be trained for war."

What a change!
The killing sword
Transformed into a tool of growth
Destructive energy transformed
Serving the heart's wants
Stop the war!

Discrimination
The sword swung in service of life
Clarity emerges within
No more killing Self

What to grow?
Plant your heart's desires
Nurture what's desired, prune the rest
Plowshares and pruning knives grow life
Your soul manifests

IMAGINE THE NATION of _____ (fill in your name). Your habit patterns, beliefs, and desires, and thought processes are the states of the nation. How often do you experience a war inside yourself? One internal state wants one outcome while another wants something different. The path of salvation (a.k.a. enlightenment or individuation) leads to a state of peace that underlies whatever chaos or unrest we experience. In the process, tools of destruction are transformed into tools of creation. The war against our selves ends; killing energies are turned into agents of growth.

A seed of God Within exists within all our patterns of behavior, even the destructive, self-sabotaging ones. We access the Divine seed through our felt sense. When we connect to the emotion and body sensations of the felt sense accompanying our behavior, we invite a transformation of the energies inherent in the behavior. A new pattern can form. Something previously used for killing, like a sword, can be changed into an agent of creation, like a plowshare.

For instance we may have a strong dislike for a behavior, attitude, or being state. The dislike could become an agent of destruction through self-condemnation that berates, shames, and paralyzes. The result would be depression, worthlessness, and inertia. If used as an agent of creation, the dislike could prompt us to connect with the desire to do something differently. The desire to act differently, think differently, or be different has to be present or the dislike would not surface. Disliking a behavior is different than disliking one's Self. When we can relate to our felt sense with the knowledge that there is more to us than just one feeling, we can connect to the energy and use it to cultivate what is desired. The dislike then destroys an undesirable behavior, not the self. Perhaps, this is what it means that a sword becomes a plowshare.

I often think the work of consciousness is like gardening. We have to till the soil, plow the rows, sow the seeds, pull the weeds, fertilize the plants, and reap the harvest. Each of these steps must occur at just the right time in the cycle of growth. Our soul's manifestation is the same. We have seasons of growth. The ego/self can let things grow unattended, or we can consciously participate in the growth process by being in relationship to God Within. When we choose being in relationship, we invite the transformation that leads to peace within the "nation" we are.

NOTES

One: This scripture is seen as a prophecy of the characteristics of the new age known as "The New Jerusalem." It is also associated with the birth of Jesus the Christ and the second coming of Christ. Psychologically, the scripture speaks to the opus of individuation—an ego consciously living in sync with the Self or God Within. Symbolically, the New Jerusalem is a state of integration; wholeness is the result. Whenever we experience a unifying of opposing energies within our self, we experience the peace and transformation referenced in the scripture. We have an experience of the new age within us.

Two: Although we think of the sword as a weapon of destruction, it is a symbol for the psychological function of discrimination.

CHAPTER 9

FINDING GOD IN SEEMING EVIL:
Job 1:1–10

From the cross, Jesus uttered, "My God, my God, why hast thou forsaken me?" We too sometimes feel abandoned by God Within. When we feel wronged by God or the Self, it serves us well to look for what and how the forces of destruction, creation, and integration are moving within us.

Verse 10, "'If we accept good from God, shall we not accept evil?' Throughout all this, Job did not utter one sinful word."

THE IDEA OF A GOD that is author of both good and evil is distasteful to many people. Yet, today's scripture makes it clear that all comes from God. Psychologically, the Self is the manifestation of God within our psyches. C. G. Jung wrote, "The Self is the originator of that which is both helpful, and injurious to the self." When we grasp that all we think, feel, say, and experience has a seed of God Within in it, we are able to move beyond the surface appearance that may appear "evil" to the unseen energies and dynamics at play.

The Kabbalistic definition of evil is "misapplied force." Misapplied force means using an energy in a way that is opposite of what is needed or how it is intended. For instance, a heap of coals in the fireplace is "good," a heap of coals on a rug is "evil."

Whether we use something in service of life or against life determines whether it is evil. Coals in the fireplace serve life; coals on the rug only burn the rug! Anger that prompts a change in our action serves life; anger that feeds rage keeps us stuck as it destroys the movement prompted by the emotion.

The dynamics of destruction, creation, and integration are always working in and around us. They are at work in our body's metabolism, which includes anabolic (building up) and catabolic (destroying) phases. Both are necessary for the synthesis or integration of new cells. These dynamics are present in our lives on all four planes: physical, emotional, mental, and spiritual. When we understand that something old must go in order for something new to come, we can align with the life cycle of creation, destruction, and integration. We can use whatever appears within us—usually as a sensation, emotion, or desire prompting an image, thought, or impulse—in sync with the appropriate phase of the cycle.

When we feel God or the Self has wronged us, it can serve us well to look for what and how the forces of destruction, creation, and integration are moving within us. Are we expressing emotion to create our heart's desires or to inadvertently thwart and "destroy" them? Do our thoughts create images that reflect our heart's desires or stifle them? Do we align with the totality of God Within or do we judge some expressions and dismiss them?

Inner Reflection

Take a few moments to reflect on what is being created in your life and what is being destroyed. Ask the Self/God Within to show you the life cycle at work so that you may see beyond what seems "evil" and respond to the energy within you in service of your Inner Divine Spirit.

CHAPTER 10

TRANSFORMATION FROM DEATH:
Isaiah 6:1–8

Resurrection is the ultimate goal of death. Something dies and something new is born. The story of Jesus' death and his resurrection as the Christ offer us the truth of transformation. New life comes on the heels of destruction.

Verse 1, "In the year of King Uzziah's death, I saw the Lord…"

Verses 6-7, "Then one of the seraphim flew to me carrying in his hand a coal which he had taken from the altar with a pair of tongs. He touched my mouth with it and said, 'See, this has touched your lips; your iniquity is removed, and your sin is wiped away.'"

ISAIAH'S EXPERIENCE of seeing the Lord begins with the death of King Uzziah. The conditions under which Isaiah's encounter occurred started with an ending, a passing, a death. In the space of a loss, Isaiah saw the Lord enthroned. Isaiah had a moment of clarity and declared, "Woe is me. I am lost, for I am a man of unclean lips." The seraphim responded to his self-reflection, self-awareness, and acknowledgment of his internal sense of self. He was touched by the seraphim and cleansed of sin. His acceptance of God's call begins.

When we think symbolically, Isaiah's story gives a picture of the internal, organic process of transformation (change) in our lives. The start of change occurs when something dies; usually, we notice something's changing because of a shift in emotions and feelings. The change may be a passing of an attitude or belief, feeling or passion, or action or habit. It may be reflected in the outer world as a difference in relationships or environment.

In the process of transformative loss, we encounter the larger Self who expresses through all we feel, think, and experience. We are touched by God Within bringing something new. We experience a burning passion or desire that is not of the ego's choosing or bidding. We feel changed by this passion—cleansed, released from something old, desirous of something different for our selves. We become willing to follow the heart's desire and let it energize and move us. We follow the new found sense of connection to God Within. We act on it.

In Jungian psychology, the seraphim symbolize an archetype, a universal template of an energy that has feeling characteristics and qualities common among all peoples (examples include Mother, Father, Inferiority, Superiority). Archetypes are born in us, as they are part of our human nature. Archetypes are often experienced as numinous, spirit-like, and larger than life as they tend to present through emotions and felt-sense experiences that are unbidden. Archetypes set in motion behaviors that occur throughout the lifespan.

The most important thing to know is that we are born with energies and resources that the archetypes represent. **They respond to our self-reflection, self-awareness, and acceptance of feelings of being lost, not knowing, inadequacy, wrongdoing, and sinfulness.**

We tend to deny, dismiss, and fear loss. We do not like not knowing or acknowledging what we do not see clearly. We tend to fear change because of the unknown ending and beginning. Our acceptance of our unknowingness, which we often feel as being lost, is what prompts the archetypes within us to come to our aid. We have to realize and acknowledge our ego limitations in order to receive help from the touch of the God Within. △

Inner Reflection

Take a few moments to reflect on what is dying/changing in your life. Acknowledge whatever feelings of loss and lack of direction or unknowingness you feel in the face of the situations. Open to experience the touch of God Within however it comes (emotion, desire, felt sense, and so forth). Move as your inner Divine knowing prompts.

Note:

The Greek word for sin is an archery term for "missing the mark." Sin means our self-expression is missing the mark of reflecting and expressing God Within.

CHAPTER 11

OUR COMPLETION:
Colossians 2:8–23

The lower nature of humanity is seen many times in the Easter story. Greed, self-preservation, lying, violence, and misguided ideas surround the betrayal and death of Jesus. We all have instinctive, reflexive reactions that harm us and others. We become more whole as we see through the automatic, "blind" responses of emotions, urges, impulses, and compulsions to the seed of the Divine Within that is seeking expression.

Verse 9, 11, "For it is in Christ that the complete being of the Godhead dwells embodied, and in him you have been brought to completion… In him also you were circumcised, not in a physical sense, but by being divested of the lower nature; this is Christ's way of circumcision."

PSYCHOLOLGICALLY, to be in Christ means to have a sense of oneness with our essential nature or larger Self, which is the totality of our psyche/soul. As a symbol, Christ connects us to the larger Self that holds all aspects of our nature, which is an extension of God.

The Tree of Life from Kabbalah shows the energy of God flowing as the life force into Divine Soul. The Divine Soul flows into the Ruach, the Breath of God Within. Here, we know oneness with our essential nature, which is "like unto God". We feel and experience the beauty and balance of our Divine soul. Some people refer to this balance as the still-point or centerpoint within. The Ruach flows into our vital soul and body where we encounter the breath in our sensations, intuitions, feelings, and thoughts. Thus, "in Christ the complete being of the Godhead dwells embodied."

The vital soul, also known as our animal nature, is the lower nature. It is lower in that it operates below the surface of consciousness. Our ego has no will or control over it. The vital soul is the life force as it manifests in automatic, reflexive, and instinctive responses with no space or pause for self-awareness or self-reflection before a body sensation or impulse is expressed in behavior. All automatic, reflexive responses originate from inborn tendencies and learned/conditioned response patterns.

The lower nature is most often associated with the instincts of hunger, sexuality, and activity of self-preservation. Satisfaction of these urges is basic and necessary for healthy living. They become problematic only when we displace other needs into these instincts. Some examples of this displacement include seeking sex when we really desire emotional and spiritual closeness or overeating when we need emotional nourishment.

The scripture says that Christ circumcised the lower nature, divested it. He did not cut it off, condemn it, or deny it. Webster's first definition of divest is "to undress or strip." In circumcision, the foreskin of the penis is removed; the penis or phallus is uncovered, unhidden, not removed. Circumcision of our lower nature means removing the covering of the unconscious, so we see behind the automatic, "blind" responses of emotions, urges, and impulses.

The circumcision or divesting of our lower or unconscious nature requires us to pay attention and become aware of the feelings and meanings behind our felt senses. When we see beyond the surface want or impulse or urge, we can choose a response other than the inborn or conditioned one. We see our inner workings from the viewpoint of our totality or God Within instead of from our adaptive personality self. We then begin to experience the "complete being of the Godhead" within us.

Inner Reflection

Take a few minutes to identify an automatic pattern of response that is problematic. Open to seeing it from new angles. Ask God Within to divest it and show you the true need or yearning it holds. Stand with the totality of who you are and let this move you into action.

CHAPTER 12

FOLLOWING THE INNER DIVINE:
Matthew 4:18–22, Romans 10:8b–18

Many times in his ministry, Jesus withdrew to be alone for prayer. He sought the knowing that comes only from hearing the still, small voice of God Within. He listened and followed even to death. As we speak our prayers, we hear what is in our heart. As we listen, we hear the deeper Voice of Silence that is God Within.

Matthew 4:22, "He [Jesus] called them, and at once they [James son of Zebedee and his brother John] left the boat and their father, and followed him."

Romans 10:10, "For the faith that leads to righteousness is in the heart, and the confession that leads to salvation is upon the lips."

Leaving the well known
Familiar that launched us
Divine Self requires it
Our call comes from within

Following the Self
A path that's only ours
Divine Authority
Found in depths of our heart

Courageous James and John
Jesus called; they followed
Shifting their allegiance
Outer to Inner

Our heart knows our path
Whispering soul's longing
God's Presence within
Calls and guides

OUR HEART KNOWS our path. So often, we search outside for something that is found only within. In Jung's work with patients, he found that people are the healthiest and most well adjusted when they live in the flow of their soul's (psyche's) energy. Jung believed that the soul/psyche has a gradient it naturally follows unless blocked. Our psychic energy flows outward in our body sensations, intuitions, thoughts, and feelings. **When we pay attention to what goes on inside our body and mind, we encounter our living soul.**

Symbolically, the heart is the seat of our emotions and our passions. We speak of what is in the heart as referencing the deepest longings of our soul. Our heart speaks to us in our felt experiences. We know the stirrings of the Divine first in our gut. Then, we access words to harness what we know experientially. In such moments, we encounter The Voice of Silence—the still, small voice of God that informs us. We feel peace, order, and "rightness" that are beyond words. We are called to action on an aspect of our self/Self that is ready to be lived.

The larger Self, or totality of psyche which reflects Christ, is always prompting us. God Within calls us to live more fully who we are. We speak our soul's truth. Sometimes we realize this, other times we dismiss it. We have only to listen to our heart's knowing and hear what comes from within; the "confession that leads to salvation is upon the lips." God Within knows what is next in our journey towards wholeness or salvation.

Inner Reflection

I invite you to listen to yourself today. What is "the confession upon your lips"? What are you saying about yourself that has the potential to connect you more consciously with your heart's desires? Where are you acknowledging your soul's movement? Where are you dismissing it inadvertently?

Take a few minutes to quiet your mind, open your heart, and listen for the call of the Divine Within. Make this a daily practice. The more we follow the call, the more easily we hear it.

CHAPTER 13

LAYING DOWN YOUR LIFE:
1 Kings 5:1–6:1

Easter is the story of Jesus the man willingly laying down his life to be resurrected as the Christ. We are called to lay down our life for our friends by giving up the preconceived ideas we project onto them. By owning what is within us instead of putting it on them, we move towards the wholeness of the Christ as we integrate all aspects of God Within.

Verses 12-15a, "This is my commandment, that you love one another as I have loved you. There is no greater love than this, that a man should lay down his life for his friends."

PSYCHOLOGICALLY, to lay down our life for another means to let go of who we think we are in relationship and be open to what we are experiencing in the moment, including how we are impacting the other. Our ego consciousness—who we think we are and how we perceive —is only one aspect of the Self that is present. To every interaction, we bring all aspects of our psyche—what we know and what we do not know about (our conscious and unconscious selves).

Love is relational. Whenever we feel love, there is always an object or recipient of the love. The object may be another person, a pet, a feeling, an activity, nature, or a thing. Regardless, love binds. It draws us towards someone or something. It connects.

Jung writes that the "need for human connection," what he calls kinship libido, is always present. We want human connection so much that we filter, censor, and edit who we are so we feel acceptable to others. Our ego/sense of self survives by disowning parts of our psyche/soul (i.e., thoughts, emotions, talents) that do not coincide with who we think we should be according to external standards (i.e., family, church, the other person).

Denied aspects of our self tend to become filters through which we experience others. We end up attributing our unconscious thoughts and feelings to someone else. We project them onto another. Think about how a movie projector works. Your unconscious psyche is the machine and the other person is the screen.

To lay down our life for our friend's means giving up the projections and owning what is within. We have to lay down our ideas of who we are and consciously relate to all we are. This means paying attention and relating to whatever is going on inside us. By doing this, we become capable of doing the same for another person.

Inner Reflection

To begin to reconnect with disowned or repressed aspects of your psyche/soul, pay attention to feelings of unrest and dis-ease masking guilt and shame that show up when thoughts, emotions, and desires begin to stir. Practice extending the arms of love— acknowledgment, acceptance, recognition, validation, and gratitude--to whatever shows up. (See *The Four Fold Way* by Angeles Arrien). Ask God Within to give you the courage to lay down your projections and see the truth of who you are.

CHAPTER 14

ACTION REQUIRED, PART 1: FAITH
2 Peter 1:1–11

The scriptures tell us that Jesus spent time preparing himself before he began his public ministry. He made choices along the way to stay rooted in what he knew his path to be. He exemplified the qualities of faith, virtue, knowledge, self-control, fortitude, piety, brotherly kindness, and love. We are called to cultivate these qualities within our nature. When we use our psychological functions of thinking, feeling, sensation, and intuition to develop these qualities, we are choosing to strengthen our connection to God Within/Self.

Verses 5-7, (NEB) "With all this in view, you should try your hardest to supplement your faith with virtue, virtue with knowledge, knowledge with self-control, self-control with fortitude, fortitude with piety, piety with brotherly kindness, and brotherly kindness with love."

(RSV) "For this very reason make every effort to add to your faith goodness; and to goodness knowledge, and to knowledge, self-control; and to self-control, perseverance; and to perseverance, godliness, and to godliness, brotherly kindness; and to brotherly kindness, love. For if you possess these qualities, they will keep you from being ineffective and unproductive in your knowledge of our Lord Jesus Christ."

WHAT A LIST of qualities to develop! I have studied them for months now. The result is a series of mediations considering each quality. I see the states of consciousness that each quality represents as building blocks on our path of individuation/salvation. Each block is a foundation for the next; one quality cannot be present without the preceding one. Today's meditation addresses the call to action and the aspect of faith that is tied to our personal relationships.

The path of individuation/salvation requires action. We do not consistently expand our consciousness without focusing will. Will is the accessible power to channel our energies in a certain direction. With the power to choose, we also need the presence of love as it binds things together. Love in the form of compassion brings an integration of our energies in service of life. What we desire and access with will comes to us!

Faith is the beginning of all acts of attention. The first definition of faith given in *Webster's New Collegiate Dictionary* is "allegiance to duty or a person; loyalty; fidelity to one's promises." The second definition is "belief and trust in and loyalty to God; firm belief for something in which there is no proof; complete confidence." Our loyalties and our beliefs become organizing forces of our sense of self, how we move, and how we relate to self and other. Our libido, or life force, automatically shapes itself into patterns of response that follow the expectations or law of others who matter most to us. As children, the family system is the first purveyor of the duties and responsibilities by which we move. We unconsciously adapt to our families' ways of being and doing.

In the process of adaptation, we may develop a mask, or false self, that we show the outside world. The mask is aligned with outer-world expectations; it may or may not reflect the truth of our larger Self. We may ignore or silence the voice of God Within in order to be safe, to be accepted, or to feel loved. We unknowingly adapt a way of motivating our selves related to the outside world and outer relationships. We may set aside or ignore the promptings of our heart and larger Self if these promptings are different from the outer expectations. "Should, must, and ought to" thoughts are markers of an adaptive self. They indicate living from the head with laws instead of living from the felt energy of the larger Self/God Within.

Knowing to whom and to what we are loyal is a first step towards knowing our faith. Our words and ideas may say one thing; but, our actions show the deeper truth of our *modus operandi*. As we see our allegiances, our loyalties, and our promises in action, we begin to access the will needed to cultivate faith in God Within.

Inner Reflection

Invite a compassionate attitude as you look to see the nuances of your daily loyalties, allegiances, and promises. Where do you spend your energy physically in action, emotionally in feeling, mentally in your thoughts, and spiritually in your sense of being? What do you value in your daily choices?

As you see your faith as evidenced in your allegiances, sense of duty, and loyalties, your heart can inform you as to their truth for you now. Let this knowing shape your actions.

CHAPTER 15

ACTION REQUIRED, PART 2: FAITH

2 Peter 1:1–11

Jesus prayed in the Garden of Gethsemane as he struggled with the knowledge of what was to happen to him. He went to the source of his faith, his own experience of God, with his unrest. Our journey towards wholeness involves many changes. As we follow our experience of God and act on our faith, we also need to return to the source, God Within, with our struggles.

Verses 5-7, (NEB) "With all this in view, you should try your hardest to supplement your faith with virtue, virtue with knowledge, knowledge with self-control, self-control with fortitude, fortitude with piety, piety with brotherly kindness, and brotherly kindness with love."

(RSV) "For this very reason make every effort to add to your faith goodness; and to goodness knowledge, and to knowledge, self-control; and to self-control, perseverance; and to perseverance, godliness, and to godliness, brotherly kindness; and to brotherly kindness, love. For if you possess these qualities, they will keep you from being ineffective and unproductive in your knowledge of our Lord Jesus Christ."

THE SECOND DEFINITION of faith in *Webster's New Collegiate Dictionary* is "belief and trust in and loyalty to God; firm belief for something in which there is no proof; complete confidence." This level of faith requires trust in our felt experience over the stated beliefs of others. We may pay lip service to a faith that states certain beliefs because we have been taught that is truth. However, faith that comes from an embodied experience where we encounter the numinous is a different type of faith. The former exists in the intellect as ideas, the latter lives in the body mind as knowing.

Living an embodied faith means holding the truth of our experience. We hold onto what we know through our body mind; our felt knowledge informs our actions on every plane: physical, emotional, mental, and spiritual. No one else has our particular felt sense. We may have common shared events, but each of us has our own unique felt experience. No one else can be in our body, feel what we feel, or know what we know.

Faith is not an intellectual idea or cognitive belief. Faith is a deep knowing that comes from an experience we feel in our body mind. Dionne Fortune's definition of faith aptly describes embodied faith. She said, "faith is the conscious result of super-conscious [beyond ego, numinous/spirit filled] experience which has not been translated into terms of brain consciousness (cognitions) and of which, therefore the normal personality (our ego/self) is not directly aware, though it nevertheless feels, possibly with great intensity, the effects, and its emotional reactions are fundamentally and permanently modified thereby."

Encounters with the Divine change us. The meetings may be prompted by outer events, but we feel the shift internally. Something in our body mind recognizes The Mystery that we call

God. We feel energized by the heightened connection with the Divine Essence. We know our psyche/soul to be an expression of the Divine through us. We are changed in some way.

All great spiritual traditions include practices to facilitate an experience of God, the Mystery. Prayer, meditation, worship, song, and scripture study are some examples of such disciplines. We may or may not encounter the Divine in these ways. Many people experience the Divine when in nature. The essence of the life force that is God shines brightly through the handiworks of the natural world. The unadulterated purity of a forest or a stretch of beach connects us to the invisible realm of vibrating molecular structures. We know there is something more than meets the physical eye.

However we seek and know the Mystery, we must desire more than anything to know God in an embodied way. The realm of transformation is our personality/self. Our body mind is the field of encounter between our little self/ego and our larger Self/God Within. Seeking to know the Divine Spirit Within is the starting point. △

Inner Reflection

Let each day include a practice that invites and cultivates your openness to knowing the Divine in and around you. The practice may be as simple as feeling the life force pulse through you as you breathe. It may include mindful movement. The practice of gratitude helps you to see the Divine around you. You can say a quiet thank you before each meal. Open to see what is larger than you, your ego consciousness. In this way, you encounter God Within.

CHAPTER 16

ACTION REQUIRED, PART 3a: VIRTUE
2 Peter 1:1–11

Jesus followed what he knew to be the will of the Divine for him. He moved forward throughout his life, even to death, with an embodied faith. As we cultivate the virtues of fortitude, temperance, and prudence, we align with the flow of the life force in us. We mediate the various energies within our body and mind so we know the natural direction our soul wants to go.

Verses 5-7, (NEB) "With all this in view, you should try your hardest to supplement your faith with virtue, virtue with knowledge, knowledge with self-control, self-control with fortitude, fortitude with piety, piety with brotherly kindness, and brotherly kindness with love."

(RSV) "For this very reason make every effort to add to your faith goodness; and to goodness knowledge, and to knowledge, self-control; and to self-control, perseverance; and to perseverance, godliness, and to godliness, brotherly kindness; and to brotherly kindness, love. For if you possess these qualities, they will keep you from being ineffective and unproductive in your knowledge of our Lord Jesus Christ."

OUR HUMAN LOYALTIES and our embodied experience of the numinous are the foundation of who we are as individuals. When we know what makes us tick and how we move in the world, we have greater freedom of choice in how to act. We can begin to let go of what is not the truth of our soul; we can cultivate living in ways that more fully express our true nature. Our ability to exert willpower is increased.

Willpower is how we think we influence the way our libido/life force flows. The esoteric tradition teaches that there is no will outside the will of the Divine. This concept has created much debate throughout the centuries. Leslie Weatherhead has a wonderful book titled The Will of God that addresses three aspects of the will of God: intentional will, circumstantial will, and ultimate will. Weatherhead makes a distinction between God's ideal or intentional will, the influence of our choices and natural law in circumstantial will, and the use of circumstances for our highest good (ultimate will). It is a great read; I highly recommend it!

Analytical psychology teaches that our libido/life force has a gradient that it will follow naturally, if unobstructed. We have a path to follow that is uniquely our own. The Self, the totality of psyche/soul, holds the truth of who we are. We can think of this truth as the Divine Will in us. We know it through the desires and impulses that flow from our heart into our body and mind. These desires shape thoughts, images, and fantasies about our life. When we live the truth of our soul, we are the healthiest.

Our reflexive, instinctive responses are designed to ensure our survival. As an infant, this means belonging with the people around us. The basic need for connection to other people sets in motion patterns of accommodation. Often, we accommodate by cutting off our sensory experiences, desires, longings, etc. Loyalty to our family's way of thinking, feeling, and doing may be necessary when we are helpless and dependent children. But as adults, we may find that loyalty to childhood beliefs often shut down our own inner knowing. The inability to live congruently with our soul creates unnecessary suffering. Consciousness brings an opportunity to move beyond the suffering, if we choose our soul's truth over the familial.

We are not in charge of the flow of the life force, but we have power in how we respond. This is true for what goes on inside of us as well as outside of us. When we build a relationship to the energies within us, we establish a dialogue with our Higher Self, the God Within us, the totality of who we are. When we are loyal to our true Self, we are in the willpower that energizes, stimulates, and propels us to live our truth. This is the willpower or libido that is our birthright.

We need conscious access to the Divine Will within us to cultivate the qualities associated with virtue. Virtue can be defined as excellence or moral energy. Excellence is an expression of our Self, our Inner Divine Spirit. Our soul has a conscience that is far superior to any imposed legal order. Once we have tamed our animal nature (to which the Ten Commandments speak), we can feel our soul moving us to act with virtue.

Thomas of Aquinas, a medieval theologian, talked about the moral virtues of prudence, justice, fortitude, and temperance and described them as "settled dispositions of various appetitive powers which incline toward and allow their possessors to make good moral choices." We can think of them as good habits that we can develop. The work of consciousness helps us discern our soul's desires from the instinctive or "appetitive powers" and learned survival responses. Instinctive, survival impulses can distort, confuse, and exaggerate our needs.

Traditional church thought also defines the theological virtues of faith, hope, and charity/love and believes the Divine infuses these virtues into us. The psychological structure through which these virtues flow is the Self, the totality of our psyche/soul. By reaching for the Self, the Divine Within, we can strengthen our ability to know the promptings of our psyche/soul. We often refer to these as the desires of our heart.

Inner Reflection

Take a few minutes to reflect on what you know in your heart. Where does this knowing get short-circuited by learned patterns from the outer world? Maybe, you give up acting with your heart's prompting in order to placate someone else. Perhaps, you learned that asking for what you want or need is a burden to another even though we all need one another. How do your creative impulses get squeezed out by the inner taskmaster? Breathe deeply, and open to know the virtue, the excellence of God Within. Where do you feel the energy/the willpower to follow your heart's desires? Identify one action you can take for the next 21 days that supports you moving from the virtue of your soul.

CHAPTER 17

ACTION REQUIRED, PART 3b: VIRTUE OF PRUDENCE

2 Peter 1:1–11

In the Easter story, we see many examples of the lack of virtue. Pilate wanted to please the crowd even though he found no fault with Jesus. Peter denied knowing Jesus even though he followed him. The soldiers acted out the collective decision to kill. When we develop the virtue of prudence, we meet our intellectual, emotional, mental, and physical desires with wise discernment. We live the truth of our heart's desires and release the desires not of our heart.

Verses 5-7, (NEB) "With all this in view, you should try your hardest to supplement your faith with virtue, virtue with knowledge, knowledge with self-control, self-control with fortitude, fortitude with piety, piety with brotherly kindness, and brotherly kindness with love."

(RSV) "For this very reason make every effort to add to your faith goodness; and to goodness knowledge, and to knowledge, self-control; and to self-control, perseverance; and to perseverance, godliness, and to godliness, brotherly kindness; and to brotherly kindness, love. For if you possess these qualities, they will keep you from being ineffective and unproductive in your knowledge of our Lord Jesus Christ."

ALTHOUGH CHURCH theologians have elaborated on what Thomas of Aquinas said regarding virtues, I want to consider what they mean psychologically. After all, **the field in which we do the work of regeneration or rebirth is our personality or conscious self/ego.** Our ego is the agent through which our soul moves in the world. With our ego, we can seek to know the essence of our psyche/soul or we can ignore it. If we choose to seek, we must cultivate the virtues of prudence, justice, fortitude, and temperance.

Thomas of Aquinas elaborated on these virtues with the following pairings. We are to cultivate prudence in our practical intellect; justice with our rational appetite that we experience as our will; fortitude/courage with our irascible appetite that draws us to what is painful; and temperance/balance with our bodily appetite that draws us to what is pleasurable. So,

clearly our appetites are the focus of our work. Our appetites are the messengers of our instinctive needs and wants.

Throughout history, humans have struggled to tame their instinctive natures. So much of who we are is instinctive, meaning it is reflexive or automatic! We begin as an infant child who does not have prudence in the sense of "the ability to govern and discipline oneself by the use of reason" (*Webster's New Collegiate Dictionary's* definition of prudence). We have to develop prudence. Our ability to exercise "skill and good judgment in the use of resources" (*Webster's* next definition of prudence) is learned from outside sources as well as from our responses to our experiences of success and failure.

Unfortunately, we have used the defense mechanism of repression as a way to be prudent. The problem is that when we repress something, it is not transformed. It stays in the same state of consciousness, but it goes out of ego awareness. The energy is still in us, but it is not accessible or amenable to our conscious self. This energy has volition outside ego control and acts of its own accord. It can show up in all kinds of problematic personality traits, destructive behaviors, counter-productive actions, etc. Instead of using our intellect to repress our energies of desire (including the aforementioned appetites), we need to use our intellect to acknowledge, meet, understand, and direct our desires in line with our total Self.

When we feel any desire (appetite), we can feel as if it is all we are. In the moment, the feeling may consume us. The first necessary step towards prudence is to know we are more than any one desire. It is our intellect's job to see our specific desires in the context of our soul. Too often, intellectual reason works to maintain outer world expectations at the expense of our soul. We see this in practices of self-flagellation, self-denial, and self-sacrifice that create numbness. We need to use the capacity of intellectual reason to create thoughts, habits, structures, etc. that allow our soul's desires to live.

Our greatest resource is our libido/life force. We know our life force through the sensations of our body mind. To exercise prudence that serves the soul, we have to relate to our life force as it makes itself known in our desires. We need prudence in our intellect as it serves the soul in exercising prudence with our appetites.   △

Inner Reflection

What is your relationship to your intellect, your will, your draw to what is pleasurable, and your draw to what creates pain in your life? Does your reason dismiss your desires? Do your desires operate unconsciously? Where do you self-sabotage? Imagine reason compassionately working with your appetites to help you live the truth of your heart's desires and release the desires not of your heart.

CHAPTER 18

ACTION REQUIRED, PART 3c: VIRTUES OF JUSTICE, FORTITUDE, AND TEMPERANCE

2 Peter 1:1–11

We have a choice as to whether we live consciously in relationship to the Self/God Within, the totality of our psyche/soul. We can give our selves over to whatever comes, or we can decide which direction to move with our energies. We can go to sleep like the disciples did while Jesus was praying in the Garden, or we can stay awake. Staying awake means facing all that is in us. We need the virtues of justice, fortitude, and temperance.

Verses 5-7, (**NEB**) "With all this in view, you should try your hardest to supplement your faith with virtue, virtue with knowledge, knowledge with self-control, self-control with fortitude, fortitude with piety, piety with brotherly kindness, and brotherly kindness with love."

(**RSV**) "For this very reason make every effort to add to your faith goodness; and to goodness knowledge, and to knowledge, self-control; and to self-control, perseverance; and to perseverance, godliness, and to godliness, brotherly kindness; and to brotherly kindness, love. For if you possess these qualities, they will keep you from being ineffective and unproductive in your knowledge of our Lord Jesus Christ."

WANT TO CONSIDER the psychological work of justice, fortitude, and temperance together. These three virtues need one another to exist. Justice brings to mind getting our due, right alignment, and obedience to the law. It is about balancing two opposites. Fortitude means having stick-to-it-ness, courage, and perseverance. It implies stamina. Temperance implies a blending of qualities. The essence of one quality affects the essence of the other; the strength of one is altered by the strength of the other. We know this from chemistry (including baking) as well as from our psyche.

Psyche/soul has a built-in justice of its own in the principle of compensation. Parts of psyche complement or complete one another. The unconscious self compensates the conscious self. We see this compensation when unacknowledged emotions, feelings, or desires show up in our dreams. We also experience it in moments we blurt out feelings and thoughts we have pretended to not have. All contents of our psyche hold some amount of psychic energy or libido/life force. The energy demands to have its rightful expression. The innate process of compensation assures this expression happens.

The work of individuation brings the energy that otherwise stays unconscious into conscious awareness. As we build a relationship between our ego/conscious sense of self and the unknown/unconscious aspects of self, the negative effects of the unconscious are mitigated. Consciousness can focus to keep both views in our mind. By holding the two together in our mind, with the intention of tempering the extremes of the opposing energies, we invite the organic process known as the Transcendent Function. As a result of The Transcendent Function respond-

ing to our consciously holding the tension of opposites, a
uniting third emerges. The third
comes as an inner knowing; we
feel it in our body with cen-
teredness and peacefulness.

The entire movement
towards a conscious relationship between our ego and larger
Self requires fortitude. Jung
says, "Consciousness is *contra
naturem*." It goes against nature.
To be conscious is like swim-
ming upstream. It takes less
effort to be swept in whatever
direction the currents (of emotion, impulse, etc.) are flowing.
Tenacity, courage, and perseverance are needed to hold our self
in relationship to the currents.
We must **want** to decide which
direction to move with the
energies, rather than letting the
pull cause us to give our selves
over to whatever comes. Often,
we wait until we feel as if we
are drowning before we find the
fortitude needed to stay with
our self in relationship to our
larger Self. *The desire to hold
on to our larger Self is the only
effective weapon against being
swept away.*

The virtues of fortitude,
temperance, and justice are
essential for our individuation.
We have to desire to live consciously in relationship to the
totality of our Self, including the
Divine Essence Within. We must
make this choice consciously.
As we strengthen the relationship between self (conscious
ego) and Self (totality of psyche
and God Within), we realize the
power of our psychic energy/
libido. Instead of repressing what
it presents, we relate to it using
the needed virtues. We apply
the necessary prudence, justice,
temperance, and fortitude.

Inner Reflection

Where do you strongly feel your desire to know the larger Self in your life? Where do you forge ahead as if your ego consciousness were all there is? Where are you struggling with opposite desires? Open to see how you can employ the virtues of prudence, fortitude, justice, and temperance to help you live more fully. Set sacred intention to hold your desire to consciously live in relationship to God Within in all situations.

CHAPTER 19

ACTION REQUIRED, PART 4: KNOWLEDGE

2 Peter 1:1–11

When we seek knowledge of our embodied soul, we encounter God in the Self, the totality of our psyche/soul. As he was dying, one of the thieves crucified beside Jesus felt the truth of Jesus' presence. He had an embodied experience that prompted him to call out to Jesus. As we encounter God Within, our sense of separateness dies. We know our selves to be with the Divine in the present moment.

Verses 5-7, (**NEB**) "With all this in view, you should try your hardest to supplement your faith with virtue, virtue with knowledge, knowledge with self-control, self-control with fortitude, fortitude with piety, piety with brotherly kindness, and brotherly kindness with love."

(**RSV**) "For this very reason make every effort to add to your faith goodness; and to goodness knowledge, and to knowledge, self-control; and to self-control, perseverance; and to perseverance, godliness, and to godliness, brotherly kindness; and to brotherly kindness, love. For if you possess these qualities, they will keep you from being ineffective and unproductive in your knowledge of our Lord Jesus Christ."

ONCE WE HAVE A conscious relationship to our faith and have developed the virtues of prudence, fortitude, temperance, and justice, we have access to our psychic energy to seek knowledge. Most of us associate knowledge with book learning. The online *Merriam-Webster's Learner's Dictionary* defines knowledge as "information, understanding, or skill that you get from experience or education." Experience is the first source of knowledge; education is the second. The next definition of knowledge is "the fact or condition of being aware of something."

Experience means direct observation or participation. Our awareness comes from attention to what is. So often, we do not have knowledge of our experience because we are not tuned in to what is happening inside us. We can be so focused on the outer world that we are not aware of our felt sense in the moment. Felt sense includes feelings, thoughts, emotions, body sensations, intuitions, perceptions—all that we know from within our body mind. We must be present to our self in the moment to know what is happening.

Education is related to the Latin word *educere*, which means, "bring out, lead forth." It involves bringing out or leading one to what is already known. This happens as we learn from others as well as from our observations of our self. The idea that the needed education is outside of our selves can contaminate the process of gaining knowledge. Instead of augmenting our experience, the process of education can conflict with or dismiss our felt sense. This conflict can create a split between head knowledge and body mind knowing. Each is a type of knowledge that has a rightful place. The work of individuation seeks to hold these two together to let a uniting third that honors inner and outer knowledge emerge. When this unity happens, we feel as if everything is going right, all is in sync, we are on target.

We are often drawn to study topics that further our understanding of what goes on inside of us. When we study these topics, education leads to embodied knowledge. On the Tree of Life, Knowledge is the invisible sphere of the Divine emanation that is the rightful place of humanity. Knowledge becomes visible in those moments we experience our selves as whole. We feel a union between our known and our unknown selves. We have a sense of oneness between our ego and our soul. Our body, mind, and spirit work harmoniously. The result is we are living our life on a soul level, not the life of conditioning from family, society, culture, etc.

The highest knowledge we can seek is the knowledge of our embodied soul as this is the point of our connection with the Divine. When we seek this knowledge, we find knowledge of all that is. We know our body mind and life as an expression of God Within.

Inner Reflection

What is the knowledge you seek? How do you pursue a greater understanding of your own nature? What helps you to understand your self? Make knowledge of who you are on a soul level a priority. Seek to know God Within, the essence of who you are. Incorporate the skills of focus, contemplation, self-reflection, and active listening into your day-to-day activities. Let your experience lead to knowledge.

CHAPTER 20

ACTION REQUIRED, PART 5: SELF-CONTROL

2 Peter 1:1–11

When we think of self-control as checking our thoughts and behaviors to see if they are a true expression of soul, we see how Jesus moved through his life with self-control. He moved out of the truth of his Self even expressing anger when he turned over the tables of the money changes in the temple. He consistently acted in sync with his heart even in his walk to death.

Verses 5-7, (NEB) "With all this in view, you should try your hardest to supplement your faith with virtue, virtue with knowledge, knowledge with self-control, self-control with fortitude, fortitude with piety, piety with brotherly kindness, and brotherly kindness with love."

(RSV) "For this very reason make every effort to add to your faith goodness; and to goodness knowledge, and to knowledge, self-control; and to self-control, perseverance; and to perseverance, godliness, and to godliness, brotherly kindness; and to brotherly kindness, love. For if you possess these qualities, they will keep you from being ineffective and unproductive in your knowledge of our Lord Jesus Christ."

HOW WE BEAT our selves up with the idea of self-control! Images of out-of-control emotions, extreme behaviors, and combative words come to mind. What does self-control really mean? Does self-control mean repression, self-denial? Do we need self-control to prevent our badness from coming out? Underlying these ideas is a destructive, negative attitude toward our self that results in becoming distant from the energy we need for healthy self-control.

Perhaps a better way to think of self-control is as self-channeling or self-direction. Etymologically, control is related to words meaning, "to check, verify, authenticate." Checking our thoughts and behaviors to see if they are a true expression of our soul brings a different perspective to self-control. The idea of checking self, verifying self, and authenticating self invokes a sense of strength for

standing with the reality of our self. This checking necessitates being with self in a way that is accepting, compassionate, loving, and affirming of the truth of our embodied self.

As a spiritual practice, self-control has to do with tempering the instincts. Our instincts emerge in the automatic, reflexive ways in which we respond. Our momentary emotions and impulses are manifestations of our instincts. However, the human experience is more than instinctive. We are capable of consciousness. Consciousness brings self-reflection. Self-reflection brings freedom of choice in how we respond. The automatic emotions and impulses may be present, but we have an ability to choose how to express them.

For healthy self-control, we must verify the authenticity of our expressions against the truth of our Self, not against other people or the outside world. We are each a unique expression of the life force. The book of Genesis tells us that we are created in the image of God. We are like unto God. I think of every particle of our being as holding the essence of God. From analytical psychology, we know all that comes from within us holds a seed of the Self or God Within. All of our response patterns are rooted in the Self. As we connect with the root or seed essence of our soul in all we feel and do, we are able to live more congruently who we are. For me, this is the highest form of self-control.

Inner Reflection

How do you practice self-control? What does it mean to you? Practice relating to whatever thoughts, emotions, feelings, or intuitions arise in you by asking the questions, "Where is the seed of my psyche/soul in this? How can I express the seed energy in a life giving way?" Affirm the value of all that is in you. Practice self-control by using the energy in service of life.

CHAPTER 21

ACTION REQUIRED, PART 6: FORTITUDE

2 Peter 1:1–11

Jesus so clearly acted with courage as he willingly went with the soldiers who arrested him. Fortitude helped him stay the course. We need fortitude to face the inner as well as outer hostilities that we encounter seeking to know the larger Self/God Within.

Verses 5-7, (NEB) "With all this in view, you should try your hardest to supplement your faith with virtue, virtue with knowledge, knowledge with self-control, self-control with fortitude, fortitude with piety, piety with brotherly kindness, and brotherly kindness with love."

(RSV) "For this very reason make every effort to add to your faith goodness; and to goodness knowledge, and to knowledge, self-control; and to self-control, perseverance; and to perseverance, godliness, and to godliness, brotherly kindness; and to brotherly kindness, love. For if you possess these qualities, they will keep you from being ineffective and unproductive in your knowledge of our Lord Jesus Christ."

THE JOURNEY TOWARDS wholeness is a lifelong one that does not happen over a few months or years; it is an ongoing quest. The scripture above gives us a stepping-stone path of qualities to develop as we advance. Fortitude is necessary to stay the course.

Webster's New Collegiate Dictionary defines fortitude as "strength of mind that enables a person to encounter danger or bear pain or adversity with courage." Synonyms include courage, strength, resolution, determination, and guts. I have often said that the path of individuation/wholeness is not for sissies. Because we like to hold onto the pretty, ideal view of who we are, we suffer when we see aspects of our nature that we have ignored, minimized, or denied because they do not fit the ideal. We must want something different to willingly meet what lurks in the shadows of our psyche.

The process of growth is a series of changes—losses and gains, deaths and rebirths, beginnings and endings. Our energy takes different forms throughout our life. We need fortitude to go through these phases of transformation. All change or transformation follows the cycle of birth, death, and rebirth. Physical, emotional, mental, and spiritual growth occurs as old patterns die and new ones are created. Unwittingly, we may shut down, give up, or go mindless when we find ourselves in the discomfort and upheaval of transformation. We may identify with the pull of inertia to hold onto what is known (even when it's not working) that is a normal part of the human experience. We resist growth; we feel persecuted by the changes. When these feelings arise, we need determination to keep moving.

When we are resolute in our desire for growth, we can hold onto the urge for something more. We can reach deep within for the impulses to live more fully. Jung identified a drive to individuation in the psyche. Individuation is the process by which we shed false ways of being. We move to attitudes, beliefs, thoughts, and feelings that embody our authentic self or soul. Courage to follow the instinctive pull towards individuation (living the whole truth of who we are) connects us to the organic energy that helps us persevere in the face of obstacles. This knowing strengthens a determination to follow the promptings of God Within, even when we are weary or despairing. Fortitude gives us the strength, courage, and energy to keep going on our soul's path. ⌂

Inner Reflection

Make it a daily practice to seek the felt sense of your psyche's prompting for growth. Where are you feeling pulled towards something new? Where do you feel a deadness that is a prompting for letting go? Exercise the spiritual muscle of fortitude by standing with your self and God Within even when afraid. Be determined to speak your truth and live the beauty of your soul. Cultivate courage rooted in the resolution to be true to your psyche/soul.

CHAPTER 22

ACTION REQUIRED, PART 7: PIETY

2 Peter 1:1–11

The pious and godly seek to see, know, and experience God in all they encounter. They meet every situation, person, event, and thing as an expression of the Divine, including what they encounter in their inner world. To make meaning out of the events of Easter week, we have to seek to know God in destruction as well as creation, in death as well as resurrection.

Verses 5-7, (NEB) "With all this in view, you should try your hardest to supplement your faith with virtue, virtue with knowledge, knowledge with self-control, self-control with fortitude, fortitude with piety, piety with brotherly kindness, and brotherly kindness with love."

(RSV) "For this very reason make every effort to add to your faith goodness; and to goodness knowledge, and to knowledge, self-control; and to self-control, perseverance; and to perseverance, godliness, and to godliness, brotherly kindness; and to brotherly kindness, love. For if you possess these qualities, they will keep you from being ineffective and unproductive in your knowledge of our Lord Jesus Christ."

PIETY AND GODLINESS invoke images of devout religious practitioners; people who are loyal to the rituals and services of their chosen church. I want to offer a different view of the godliness we are called to develop. I want us to consider godliness as operative piety, seeing all things in their relation to God and receiving all things from God. The pious and godly seek to see, know, and experience God in all they encounter. They meet every situation, person, event, and thing as an expression of the Divine, including what they encounter in their inner world.

Practicing operative piety in our inner world means seeing all that happens within us as an expression of the Divine. Even the physical conditions we label diseases, the emotions we call mental illness, and the thoughts we deem shameful hold bits of God Within. All of our emotions, feelings, thoughts, sensations, perceptions, intuitions, etc. have seeds of the larger Self at their core. The purity of their energy may be buried in the undesirability of the form they take.

We have learned to label too much of our selves negatively. We have been taught to feel shame, to reject bits of our self, and to deny parts of our soul. As a result, we end up with a weakened self. We end up on automatic pilot, going through the motions of what we think we should be or do. We do not have the connection to our larger Self that energizes us.

We need to be connected to God Within. Our ego or conscious self is constantly choosing whether or not to receive the bits of Self that show up in our affects, moods, physical sensations, etc. Our responses to inner states of feeling can be godly or ungodly. We can seek to know and honor the bit of the God Within or we can reject it because it does not look like we expected.

Over the years of my work, I have observed how difficult it is for people to practice operative piety towards themselves. For most, it is easier to extend this attitude to the outside world. When it comes to what is inside us, insidious self-hatred finds sneaky ways to generate self-condemnation, self-shaming, self-judgment, or self-deprecation!

The shame keeps us separated from our self/Self. Our inner world is the place where we most need to see everything as coming from God Within. Operative piety helps us to see beyond the negative self-talk and feelings of shame. We can then encounter God Within our body mind. We can know our self as an expression of God.

Inner Reflection

Imagine greeting whatever arises inside of you as a messenger from God. Ask the pain, the longing, the impulse, the emotion, etc. to show its underbelly to you. What is underneath or behind it? What is the energy of your psyche/soul within the presenting thing? Risk practicing operative piety instead of self-condemnation towards your inner world. Ask God Within for guidance as you cultivate godliness within.

CHAPTER 23

ACTION REQUIRED, PART 8: BROTHERLY KINDNESS

2 Peter 1:1–11

As I imagine the last meal Jesus shared with his disciples, I feel the presence of brotherly kindness. All were included, even those whom Jesus knew would soon betray him. Imagine having an inner table where you meet all parts of yourself with brotherly kindness. Practicing inner compassion allows us to practice compassion with others.

Verses 5-7, (**NEB**) "With all this in view, you should try your hardest to supplement your faith with virtue, virtue with knowledge, knowledge with self-control, self-control with fortitude, fortitude with piety, piety with brotherly kindness, and brotherly kindness with love."

(**RSV**) "For this very reason make every effort to add to your faith goodness; and to goodness knowledge, and to knowledge, self-control; and to self-control, perseverance; and to perseverance, godliness, and to godliness, brotherly kindness; and to brotherly kindness, love. For if you possess these qualities, they will keep you from being ineffective and unproductive in your knowledge of our Lord Jesus Christ."

ONCE WE HAVE developed godliness in dealing with our selves, we can extend it outward in brotherly kindness. Brotherly kindness means showing affection and concern from a place of familiarity. The familiarity we all share is the human experience. Out of our interaction with our inner world as an expression of God, we develop a compassionate acceptance of our humanness. We can then extend this compassionate acceptance to others as brotherly kindness. Kindness expresses the quality of being friendly, generous, and considerate. It is natural to extend kindness to others when we feel it towards our selves.

We all struggle with the same needs and wants, as identified on Abraham Maslow's hierarchy: physical needs such as food, shelter, warmth; safety needs (both physical and psychic); love and belonging; self-esteem; and self-actualization (living the fullness of who you are). Maslow notes that we cannot have a higher level need met without the lower ones being met. For instance, it is difficult to feel loved if you do not feel safe or have your physical needs met.

As we tend our needs, we feel a kindness towards others who have the same needs. We realize that brotherly kindness increases safety and feelings of love and belonging for all of us.

Inner brotherly kindness is the starting place. We have to make room for the inner cast of characters who show up in our psyche each day. I refer to the various energies that "speak" to us internally as characters. Each promotes a desire that may or may not be congruent with what we consciously want, think, say, or do. We all know the voice that says, "I want a brownie." We also know the voice that follows. "You don't need it. You're too fat." Both energies are inside us. Both are from the larger Self. In this way, they are siblings. We have to meet each with kindness for the energies to join with our conscious intention. If we practice inner coldness, withholding, and disrespect, we only further an inner division that zaps our energy.

Λ

Inner Reflection

Where can you extend brotherly kindness to yourself today? Look for a place of inner conflict that needs the qualities of friendliness, generosity (of spirit), and consideration (by the ego). Practice kindness as you see and sow the seeds of God Within for each of these areas. Do the same in places of conflict with other people. Imagine into the needs at work for you and the other person. Let brotherly kindness shape your response.

CHAPTER 24

ACTION REQUIRED, PART 9: LOVE

2 Peter 1:1–11

Jesus consistently acted with love. Even from the cross, he expressed a loving sentiment that his persecutors be forgiven for their ignorance. He felt his oneness with humanity and God. We cannot make love happen, but we can practice the art of loving.

Verses 5-7, (**NEB**) "With all this in view, you should try your hardest to supplement your faith with virtue, virtue with knowledge, knowledge with self-control, self-control with fortitude, fortitude with piety, piety with brotherly kindness, and brotherly kindness with love."

(**RSV**) "For this very reason make every effort to add to your faith goodness; and to goodness knowledge, and to knowledge, self-control; and to self-control, perseverance; and to perseverance, godliness, and to godliness, brotherly kindness; and to brotherly kindness, love. For if you possess these qualities, they will keep you from being ineffective and unproductive in your knowledge of our Lord Jesus Christ."

THE LAST OF THE qualities in our stepping-stone list towards individuation (salvation) is love. Perhaps, it is last because love is the Mystery. The writer of 1 John (4:9) says, "God is love." Love is our desired end as we seek union with God. Psychologically, we experience union with God as harmony between our ego (conscious self) and larger Self or God Within. We feel an inner sense of unity, as inner conflicts no longer divide us.

In Thomas of Aquinas' thought, love is one of the spiritual virtues that God bestows upon people. It is not something we can develop by our efforts. It is a gift. Love, in the sense of Mystery, has an ebb and flow that is beyond our control. It comes and goes like the tides. The poets have always reminded us of the elusiveness of love (and the beloved).

The esoteric spiritual tradition teaches that love is a natural force that is as much a part of our world as gravitational attraction. Love draws things together. It has magnetic power that is bonding; it holds things together harmoniously. Differences lose their power to divide. A unity emerges that we cannot come to through reason. We can invite such a unity by consciously relating to and holding differences (inner and outer) in respectful dialogue.

I do believe that we can create an inner receptivity to love by practicing the art of loving. Erich Fromm's *The Art of Loving* is a great primer on what it means to love. I highly recommend reading it. He talks about the different kinds of love relationships we experience (chapter 2), including brotherly love, motherly love, erotic love, self-love, and love of God. Fromm notes that all love possesses the qualities of giving, care, responsibility, respect, and knowledge (p. 24). Where we love, we naturally act in these ways.

Fromm also notes that all

arts require discipline, concentration, patience, and supreme concern for mastery (pp. 100–101) We have to work at clearing the inner patterns that block love by strengthening the conscious connection between our ego and God Within. When our life force flows freely, we feel the love that is present within our true nature as a gift of God Within. As we practice giving, care, responsibility, respect, and knowledge towards our selves, we develop a strength of self that allows us to practice the art of loving with our selves and others.

The art of loving is a conscious act. The love flowing from God Within is an automatic expression. Both give us experiences of knowing our self as one with God Within.

Inner Reflection

How are you practicing love towards yourself? Identify the ways in which you act with the qualities of love that Fromm states: giving, care, responsibility, respect, and knowledge. Where do you engage in the opposite towards yourself? Where do you feel love that seems present without any effort? Offer gratitude for being touched by the Mystery. Set intention to practice the art of loving in all your relations.

CHAPTER 25

ACTION REQUIRED, PART 10: LIVING EFFECTIVELY

2 Peter 1:1–11

To encounter the risen Christ, Jesus' followers had to give up what they knew. They had to open to experiencing what they had never before encountered. We open to encounters with the Divine as we do the ego work of developing the qualities of faith, virtue, knowledge, self-control, fortitude, piety, brotherly kindness, and love.

Verses 5-7, (NEB) "With all this in view, you should try your hardest to supplement your faith with virtue, virtue with knowledge, knowledge with self-control, self-control with fortitude, fortitude with piety, piety with brotherly kindness, and brotherly kindness with love."

(RSV) "For this very reason make every effort to add to your faith goodness; and to goodness knowledge, and to knowledge, self-control; and to self-control, perseverance; and to perseverance, godliness, and to godliness, brotherly kindness; and to brotherly kindness, love. For if you possess these qualities, they will keep you from being ineffective and unproductive in your knowledge of our Lord Jesus Christ."

WANT TO REFLECT on the last sentiment in the passage stated above. "For if you possess these qualities, they will keep you from being ineffective and unproductive in your knowledge of our Lord Jesus Christ." I am struck by the words "keep you from being ineffective and unproductive in your knowledge." It seems that having knowledge does not automatically mean that we use it effectively or productively. The statement implies that we might be ineffective and unproductive with our knowledge of "our Lord Jesus Christ." Knowing does not necessarily mean acting with wisdom.

On The Tree of Life, the sphere of Wisdom (*Chokmah*) precedes the sphere of Knowledge (*Binah*). Wisdom is associated with the highway of the stars, the Zodiac, and all the powers represented therein. Knowledge is associated with the principle of limitation, repre-sented by Saturn in the Zodiac.

Knowledge limits the larger principle of wisdom into a specific form or application. Take a moment and get what that means. Knowledge is a subset of wisdom. Wisdom instructs us in a general way of doing something while knowledge applies it to a specific situation. We might liken the idea of sitting to a principal of wisdom while the different ways to sit (floor, cushion, stool, chair) are the application of knowledge. The same is true of our behaviors. The idea of creating order is a principle of wisdom, while the various types of order are applications of knowledge. A bit of knowledge narrows the kernel of wisdom into a specific application. In the process, knowledge dismisses all the other possible shapes that wisdom might take in thought, word, or deed. Wisdom contains all the possibilities; a piece of knowledge represents only one of those possibilities. It is important to realize this distinction.

Sometimes the bit of knowledge we have is true, but it is not the truth we need for forward movement in the present moment. What we know may not be all we need to know to make a change. We may need a different key, so to speak. Different keys work different doors. Each key has an ability to open access to a space. Bits of knowledge are the same. Each is like a key that opens different dimensions of experience. The problem is that we get attached to the knowledge we have as being absolute. When we feel frustrated at the lack of change we want, we tend to doubt what we know, or we feel like God or someone has failed us. Perhaps, the reality is that we do not have the right key.

Imagine that you begin to respond to your frustration, heaviness, repetitive dead-end habits, negative thinking, or any self-defeating attitude with the question, "What's the missing piece of knowledge I need to move forward?" Instead of belittling yourself and feeling ineffective, keep sorting through the keys. Open your mind and heart to the other possibilities that come as bits of knowledge. Seek what you do not know. Keep the other bits of knowledge as the pieces of the puzzle you already have in place. You are looking for the missing piece.

We have to accept our ineffectiveness without moving into judgment of our selves. Judgment dismisses the knowledge we have and stops the flow of our energy. The seed energy of judgment is discernment. Replace judgment with compassionate discernment. Compassionate discernment lets us see what we know and what we do not know. It provides a foundation to stand with our selves as we seek increased knowledge and understanding of Wisdom. The result is that we live (more) effectively.

Inner Reflection

    I invite you to set the following sacred intention for the next 21 days: "I will practice compassionate discernment to receive the bit of knowledge I need for forward movement at this time." Identify the areas in which you feel most stuck. Ask God Within to show you the missing bits of needed knowledge. Open to hear the voice of God Within that offers compassionate discernment.

CHAPTER 26

RAISED TO NEW LIFE:
Mark 2: 1-12

Being raised in new life to Christ means we can access or connect to God Within where we can transcend/rise above the immediate state of our consciousness. We can set aside the ways of expressing and presenting our selves that keep us paralyzed. We can experience the promise of the resurrection and be freed to move in new ways.

Verse 4, "Four men were carrying him, but because of the crowd they could not get to him. So they opened up the roof over the place where Jesus was, and… lowered the stretcher on which the paralyzed man was lying."

CONSIDERED symbolically, today's scripture reading offers a picture of the interplay between aspects of our psyche that are inert or paralyzed and those that are active and discriminating. Of course, there is the crowd, the massa confusa (the mass of confusion), that blocks our discriminating attempts to reach God Within for healing of our paralysis. Our innate knowing drowns in confusion when learned beliefs and attitudes negate, dismiss, or denigrate the still, small voice of God Within that comes through our felt experience. The result is inner paralysis or inertia

I imagine the four men who lower the paralyzed man to be the psychological functions of thinking, feeling, sensation, and intuition. The story instructs us to consciously utilize these four to navigate though the confusion in order to reach the Self/Divine Within. This means calling forth what we know, what we value, what we sense, and what we intuit. Starting in the moment with the basics, if that's all that's known, is potentially transformative. The basics may be as simple as: I am (name). I physically am (name the place). I feel (emotion). I want (desire). I sense (perceptual data). I have a gut sense (intuition). Even when this seems useless, it begins to help the ego identify with "the four men" who are free to move, and not the paralyzed "man" in us.

Inertia is a given in the world of form. Without it, nothing would take a shape or structure that holds. Our bodies with its automatic processes of respiration, circulation, digestion, etc.

represent the positive aspect of inertia. The inertia of form that allows God Within to flow into our personality and environment is healthy. The inertia that paralyzes our movement and stops the flow of God Within is the problem. Where we hold onto dead, lifeless ways of thinking, feeling, emoting, doing, and being, we experience the negative aspect of inertia. We get caught in forms that block us from accessing, dialoguing and moving with the essence of God Within.

We have an option other than being paralyzed. Our ego, calling upon our thinking, feeling, sensation, and intuition can take whatever paralyzes us to God Within for healing. We can call on God Within to move us out of stagnation that keeps us caught in dead forms. We can rise above our inertia, and present the paralyzed place to God Within.

Inner Reflection

Take a few minutes to identify a place where you are stuck. Call on your thinking, feeling, sensation, and intuition to clarify and bring discrimination. Acknowledge any *massa confusa* you feel and simply move beyond it with what you can discriminate. Offer your discrimination and the paralyzed place to God Within and ask for healing. Ask that Spirit may freely move in your body mind, the Kingdom of God Within.

NOTE

The Tree of Life from Kabbalah teaches that there are ten emanations or energies that extend from God to create the world soul and the soul of humanity. The tenth, culminating sphere is *Malkuth* or the Kingdom. It is the Earth and our body mind. The virtue of this sphere is discrimination. The vice is inertia. We must learn to master these two aspects of consciousness, discrimination and inertia, while in our body.

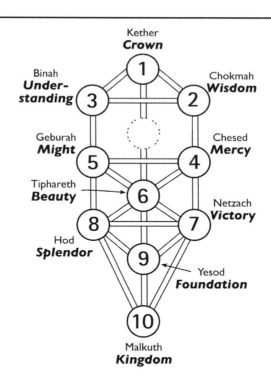

CHAPTER 27

STANDING WITH YOURSELF:
Genesis 45: 1-15

The life cycle from conception to birth to death is filled with Mystery. The story of Jesus' birth, life, death, and resurrection exemplifies the necessity of being in the moment. It is in the present moment that we can know and find God. Jospeh stayed true to God Within even when his brothers sold him into slavery. He found new life in Pharoah's household. Our ability to hold an open space, a space of unknowing, is essential in order to receive new life.

Verse 5, "Now do not be distressed or take it amiss that you sold me into slavery here; it was God who sent me ahead of you to save men's lives."

I AM STRUCK by Joseph's attitude towards his brothers. As a result of their envy, he ended up being sold into slavery and spending time in prison. In prison, Joseph used his gifts to interpret the dreams of his guards. Word of his talents spread. He was called to interpret a dream of the Pharaoh. His willingness to stand fully with himself and all he knew resulted in him becoming "a father to Pharaoh, and lord over all his household and ruler of all Egypt." (Verse 8)

We underestimate the power of standing with our inner resources and whole self. We seem to have a predisposition to noticing lack, hardship, absence, and struggle.

Like Joseph's brothers, we compare ourselves to others and we come up short. We can quickly access the guilt and shame-inducing litany of our deficits. We consciously or unconsciously may feel envy, jealousy, and hatred toward our self and/or others. Such feelings prompted Joseph's brothers to sell him into slavery. We sell ourselves when we set aside creative, life giving impulses to serve the "should's, must's, and ought to's" we tell ourselves.

The transformative energies of our psyche/soul too easily get enslaved in the mundane. We end up living according to ideals we hold in our head instead of from the essence of our being. Without realizing it, we imprison ourselves in life draining ways of being in relationship to our selves and others. We end up playing roles instead of being who we are in the moment we are. We know this is happening when we feel put upon, used, and helpless to do anything to change our situation.

Joseph gives us a beautiful example of how to move out of the state of imprisonment. We hear it expressed in his statement to his brothers, "do not be distressed...it was God..." Joseph acted with confidence in his knowing as he interpreted the dreams of the prisoners, then Pharaoh. He stood with himself even when imprisoned. He utilized his skills; he did not let go of his connection to God.

As we consciously stand with our selves by utilizing all of what we know, we begin to move out of imprisonment. We may banish parts of ourselves through denial or repression, but we have to be willing to say what's so for us (even when bits of our self are hostile to us, like Joseph's brothers were). In all aspects of our selves, the larger whole we are—God Within— keeps moving us towards wholeness and integration. Our call is to stand with all of who we are by utilizing our inner resources in every situation. △

Inner Reflection

Where do you feel imprisoned? What are the inner processes of thoughts, feelings, and sensations that keep you trapped?
How can you stand fully with yourself in these places? What
might you say? Do? How can you support yourself in cultivating
Joseph's attitude that God is in all circumstances of your life—
inner and outer? Ask God Within to give you strength to be all
that you are in service of your soul.

CHAPTER 28

EYES THAT SEE:
Luke 11:27–36

Jesus had vision that went beyond the momentary, surface appearances. His eyes saw more than the physical plane. We too have that ability. Our ego and adaptive self often interfere with our knowing by holding onto what is obvious. The seasons of Lent and Easter call us to look into the darkness with the Light of consciousness.

Verses 34-35, "When your eyes are sound, you have light for your whole body; but when the eyes are bad, you are in darkness. See to it then that the light you have is not darkness."

MUCH IS WRITTEN today about the psychology of the shadow. The idea of a dark, menacing aspect of self is intriguing. It activates the "devil made me do it" stance. It both produces and relieves anxiety as the idea of a shadow shifts responsibility from our conscious self to an "other."

The darkness of our unconscious holds what has not been developed or integrated with our consciousness. We tend to react with fear to the unbidden, the unknown, and the unseen. Our unnamed anxieties and vague feelings of mistrust get stirred, and we experience the dark as dangerous. Just what is this unknown shadow or devil that accompanies us through life?

The Western Mystery tradition associates the image of the Devil with the ideas of renewal. The Devil is known as "The

Dweller on the Threshold." It is an image of the physical world experienced only on a surface level. The image is a creature that looks absurd—chicken legs, bat's wings, and goat's horns. It is a composite of things that do not go together. It represents the mix up, distortions, and assumptions that occur when we see only what is on the surface.

When we look only with the physical eye, as if reality were flat, we meet the Devil. This is where we "have light that is darkness." Everything that is behind (or underneath) the surface is the shadow. It tends to show up in devilish ways, as it is one-sided; the shadow is not yet tempered by our conscious self and integrated with the whole of whom we are.

"Having light for your whole body" happens as we see beyond the surface. "Sound eyes" or the spiritual eye, also called the third eye, have a consciousness of the energies working behind the appearances of our behaviors or interactions. The spiritual eye sees the inward contents of emotions, desires, intentions, thoughts, beliefs, forms, and structures that create what is visible to the naked eye. Within our body mind, sound eyes strive for an awareness of the feelings, emotions, perceptions, fantasies, etc. that show up in our thoughts, feelings, and actions. The act of conscious awareness brings the light of transparency to us. We then have "light for our whole body."

Meeting the shadow—the split-off, repressed parts of our nature that show up in unbidden, undesirable forms is necessary to bring light or consciousness to our embodied self. The shadow is no longer shadow when we see it with the light of consciousness. There will always be a dance of light that casts shadows. Light and dark coexist. With sound eyes, we seek to meet the unknown or darkness in every moment.

△

Inner Reflection

Where and with what are you struggling today? What are the unknowns or "devils" that keep plaguing you? Cultivate sound eyes by looking within yourself to see the nuances of emotion, feeling, belief, thought, sensation, etc. that are present around this dark place.

As you remember the dark exists next to the light, it can be helpful to draw a mandala using symbols of color, word, or image that hold all the aspects of self. What you love and what you hate can inform one another in helpful ways when they co-exist!

CHAPTER 29

STRENGTHENED IN YOUR INNER BEING:
Ephesians 3:14–21

Our inner being is the conduit through which the Divine flows into us. Christ connects us to the Self. The great Mystery of the Easter story is to know our selves resurrected from the darkness of feeling separate from God. We are one with God. We seek to know and feel the unity in our body mind as we remember that God Within strengthens our being.

Verses 16-17, "I pray that according to the riches of his glory, he may grant that you may be strengthened in your inner being with power through his Spirit, and that Christ may dwell in your hearts through faith, as you are being rooted and grounded in love."

WE HEAR SO MUCH in pop psychology and spirituality about the secret of how to be successful in life. All too often, the teachings leave out the essential connection for change or growth. The key is the relationship between our conscious self and our larger, unconscious Self. The larger Self is our point of connection with God Within, the source of our life force or libido. By building a conscious relationship between our ego and God Within, we are energized and pulled to grow into our fullness. This is the starting point for healthy, successful living. When we recognize that the source of our energy or libido is God Within, we initiate an opening for the ego/self to more fully and clearly align with the Self. We are strengthened "in our inner being with power through God's Spirit."

Can you imagine praying for yourself daily to be "strengthened in your inner being with power through Christ's Spirit"? **What an affirmation of the reality that our inner being is the conduit for the Divine to flow into us!** Prayer sets sacred intention that focuses our attention and energies. It is a starting point for inviting God Within to be made known to our consciousness. When we greet our thoughts, feelings, sensations, and intuitions as expressions of the Divine Self, we are able to see and understand their purpose and place. We open to hear the message they carry from God Within.

In analytical psychology, Christ connects us to the Self or God Within. When we seek to see all that is within us as expressions of the Divine, we connect to the life force that sustains us. We open to moments of faith. I define faith as experiences of God Within that are not yet translatable into words but that nonetheless affect and change us. The result is that we know the presence of Christ in our hearts.

Inner Reflection

Take a few minutes to pray, in your way, to be "strengthened in your inner being with power through Christ's spirit." Feel the connection to God Within in all your thoughts, desires, feelings, etc. The conscious you is an expression of the larger you, God Within. Identify a way to remind yourself of this knowing. You can even put yellow sticky notes around your house saying, "How am I expressing God Within in this moment?" Affirm whatever you are experiencing as an expression of God Within.

CHAPTER 30

ETERNAL LIFE:
1 John 5:9–13

Christ, as the new Adam, focuses us on our inner reality and our oneness with God Within. Our conscious attention to living a unified relationship between our ego and God Within leads to a knowing of eternal life. We live through the cycles of birth, death, and resurrection that happen in our psyches/souls to experience the truth of the Easter story as we are given new life.

Verses 11, 12b, "The witness is this: that God has given us eternal life, and that this is found in his Son…he who does not possess the Son of God has not that life."

THE ESOTERIC (not mainstream) Judeo-Christian tradition teaches that humanity is the Son of God. We read in the New Testament that Jesus the Christ was the "new Adam." Adam, in Hebrew, means humanity. In the Old Testament stories, Adam/Humanity is concerned with the establishment of God as One in the outer world. In the New Testament, the new Adam/Christ focuses us on our inner reality and the oneness of our essence in our larger Self or God Within.

Consider the commandments of "Love the Lord your God with all your heart, soul, and mind; and Love your neighbor as yourself." Our relationship within, to our selves, and to God, is primary. Tending the inner realm leads to knowing the eternal life of the Divine Self that expresses through our ego/personality.

At the time of creation, humanity was given dominion over all things on earth. Adam was "put in the garden of Eden to till it and care for it" (Genesis 2:15). He was also given the responsibility and power to name the living creatures on earth (Genesis 2:19). Psychologically, the Garden of Eden is the state of consciousness where we know oneness with God Within. Our call is to cultivate this connection by naming what appears (emotions, sensations, feelings) within the psyche/soul and looking for how God Within is expressing in our felt experience.

On The Tree of Life, a "blueprint" of the emanations or aspects of God as they flow into the soul, the emanation of Adam/Christ corresponds to the Ruach, the Breath of God. The Breath of God flows through us in our breath. We associate breath with the life force or our essence. This essence keeps us alive while we are embodied. It is this essence that is eternal.

How do we experience and know the eternal essence within us? Earlier in the scripture passage referenced above, the author writes, "for there are three witnesses; the Spirit, the water, and the blood." The Spirit flows into us as the *Ruach*—the Divine Spirit that is beyond words, forms, and images. We know Spirit through our felt sense. It literally flows through the water and blood in our bodies, bringing physical and energetic nourishment to every cell of our being. Psychologically, we feel the water as our emotions and the blood as our passions. These convey the eternal God Within.

Often, our emotions, reactions, and body sensations are conditioned responses programmed by earlier experiences. Conditioned responses are not the truth of who we are as a larger Self; they reflect nuances in our personal history.

When we operate as if what we have always known and thought about our self is the total truth, we foreclose knowing God Within now.

When we open to all we are, we find life eternal. We can give up habits, patterns of thinking, being "just the way we are," to risk feeling, thinking, and acting in new ways that are expressions of God Within. We consciously own and integrate emotions, yearnings, etc. that we have previously pushed away. When we look for the seed of God Within the emotion, thought, etc., we begin to know and trust the larger Self in the face of shifting self-expressions and relationships. We know the oneness of God Within our body mind.

Inner Reflection

Begin to be aware of what is transitory in your nature and what is constant. Look for the seed of the God Within all of your expressions. Open to feel and know the oneness of Self that holds and provides a foundation within, a sense of self that lets you move and grow without fear of death/change—to know that your essence always survives.

CHAPTER 31

THE LIGHT OF LIFE:
John 8:12–20

We have the light of life when we live in conscious relationship to God Within. Jesus said, "No follower of mine shall wander in the dark." When we connect to Christ within our nature, we see the larger Self, the totality of our psyche. We realize that new life has been growing in the dark, dying places. Just as the light of spring brings new growth, the light of consciousness brings new life to our body minds.

Verse 12, "Once again Jesus addressed the people: 'I am the light of the world. No follower of mine shall wander in the dark; he shall have the light of life.'"

UNIVERSALLY, LIGHT is associated with experiences of the Divine Mystery. The Western Mystery tradition teaches that the life force (also known as libido or chi) is synonymous with Consciousness. God Within flows through all levels of our psyche—our self-consciousness, "sub" or "un" consciousness, and "supra" or transcendent consciousness.

Self-consciousness is awareness and psychic energy connected to our ego. It includes our sense of self and our abilities to do things at will (when we want). Sub- or unconsciousness includes psychic energy that our experiences in the world have conditioned and shaped into patterns of body response, emotion, thought, and action. The center of each of these patterns is a feeling associated with a universal template of energy known as an archetype. The archetype represents a psychic energy that evokes certain feelings and responses due to the qualities inherent in the archetype. (For example, the archetypes of Good Mother or Bad Mother have universal associations.) Supra, or transcendent, consciousness refers to the psychic energy of the Self/God Within.

Jesus called people to move beyond relating to God through laws or commandments that keep instinctive desires in the dark. His invitation is for us to move toward a (self) conscious knowing of our inner psychic processes, including fantasies, dreams, emotions, and reflexive responses. When we are blind to subconscious and unconscious contents, ignoring them because we fear the unknown, we move through our life in the dark. We do not see what is real, present, and active in the background of our known feelings, thoughts, and actions.

When we are aligned with God Within, our self-conscious awareness can differentiate reflexive, instinctive, biologically based impulses from the promptings of our soul. God Within speaks in our desires and feelings in ways that go beyond conditioned, predetermined responses. We see more clearly the whole of who we are, what we want, and how our life force wants to move. With the light of consciousness, we can respond to our emotions, feelings, and thoughts in different ways. With the Light of Christ, we can look to see the roots of habits and moods; we can effectively move toward different ways of being. We find the "light of the world" through God Within.

Inner Reflection

Where do you desire Light in your life? Take a few minutes to identify where you feel stuck, lost, or in the dark. Ask God Within to open your eyes to see what is present consciously and subconsciously, without blame or judgment. Track the progression of affect, thought, feeling, and action that happens internally in this place. Be open to God Within bringing Light that shows a new, more life-giving path.

CHAPTER 32

DO NOT BE AFRAID:
Matthew 14:22–33

Jesus cried out to God from the cross. He uttered his feelings. He spoke his embodied truth. The disciples cried out when they saw the unknown figure of Jesus coming towards them on the water. We too need to cry out to the Self/God Within with our deepest feelings.

Verses 27, 30-31a, "(The disciples) cried out in terror, 'It is a ghost!' But at once (Jesus) spoke to them and said: 'Take heart! It is I; do not be afraid...'...But when (Peter) saw the strength of the gale he was seized with fear; and beginning to sink, he cried, 'Save me, Lord.' Jesus at once reached out and caught hold of him."

Fear sinks
At least Peter had the courage to try
Do we?

We can call out for help
God Within always catches hold of us
Do we ask?

Self and self
Catching hold of self with Self
Do we know the difference?

OUR EGO TASK is to cultivate a conscious relationship to all within us. The all is an expression of the Self, the psychic structure that holds the essence of God Within our body mind. We sometimes move away from God Within because bits of our self appear ghostly. We do not know if what we feel is real or not. We wonder if it is from our world or another. We are scared by the unfamiliar nature of how unknown aspects of Self appear.

Our willingness to risk relating to what shows up is paramount. We can turn away in fear, or we can look more closely to see what is coming towards us. The disciples cried out in terror, and Jesus responded. We too often muffle our cries and thwart our expressions of fear. We need to cry out to the God Within to remember the totality of who we are. Our fearful ego is only one state of who we are. There is more to who we are as a whole.

Inner Reflection

Where are you encountering unknowns that trigger your fear or desperation? What is coming towards you from the outside world? What are you avoiding in your self? What are the feelings that seem too scary to acknowledge? Give voice to them now. Put them in words or sounds. Write them in your journal or verbalize out loud. Call out to your larger Self, God Within, for clarity, assurance, courage, and new life.

CHAPTER 33

OPENING TO DEATH OR CHANGE:
Mark 8:27–9:3

Form or matter (including the physical body) is not the essence of the life force. The essence of the life force is the consciousness of God Within. We get confused. We think the form (of beliefs, attitudes, habits, patterns) is what is holy. Jesus' death and resurrection remind us that the Divine is always bigger than what's known in the moment. Death is an opening for birth.

Verse 33, "(Jesus to Peter), "Away with you Satan, (he said); you think as men think, not as God thinks."

THIS SCRIPTURE is one typically read during Easter week. It reminds us that welcoming death is not an easy thing to do! We fear change and loss. Like Peter, we do not want to lose the embodiment of whom and what we value. We forget that form or matter (including the physical body) is not the essence of the life force.

The essence of the life force is the consciousness within us that is an expression of the Ruach, the breath of God. The Breath of God flows through us in our physical, mental, emotional, and spiritual bodies. Our physical bodies are the outer covering, the clothes, or cloak that house the Ruach in our psyche/soul. Our emotional temperament, our mental states, and our spiritual energetic disposition also clothe or cloak aspects of God Within. When we hold on to the external cloaks, the outer forms, over the Ruach, we lose sight of God Within.

Throughout our life span, we undergo little "deaths." Our bodies change; our minds develop; our values and desires shift; relationships come and go; our environments differ. In every change, God Within remains present and creates new, life-sustaining forms. The new forms include body cells, thought patterns, feeling states, beliefs, desires, relationships, abilities, etc. When we believe that change is wrong or bad, we cling to what is no longer necessary or life giving. This clinging blocks the flow of energy and the emergence of what is life giving and sustaining for the present.

The Christian message is one of Regeneration—birth, death, and resurrection (rebirth). We know from our sciences that this cycle is constantly at work in nature and in our bodies. Cells die each day, and new cells are born. We see this clearly as a cut or abrasion heals on the skin. Some intrusion interrupts the continuity of the skin, the body sends blood to the area, the wound clots, a scab forms, and healing goes on from underneath the skin's surface. In a few days, new skin is formed; there is a "rebirth."

Jesus knew the truth of the life cycle in a far deeper and wider way than we, or collective humanity, know. Our collective beliefs create and reinforce fears that keep us stuck in the known, familiar ways of being and living even when they have become harmful and destructive to us. We hold on to that which is no longer life giving out of a fear that there will be nothing better. We may have a belief (conscious or unconscious) that we do not deserve any better, or we may feel and act as if we are powerless to do anything differently. We can lose all we have, even our self, when we identify with and make choices from these fears.

The paradox is that in letting go of what is dying in our

life we do not lose, we find. We are "reborn" in that we receive an infusion of libido/life force as God Within is freed from old, deadening ways. We gain clearer access to the Spirit that can move us to create new, life-creating and sustaining patterns of choice and action. We experience God Within born anew in our body mind, relationships, and environment.

Inner Reflection

I invite you to reflect on your attitudes and feelings about death in all its forms. Start with the little "deaths" you have experienced as you grew from infancy to adulthood. How do you remember these changes? Do you embrace your growth or do you dread it?

Consider what in your life is dying at this time. Open to see and know God Within the structure or form (belief, habit pattern, relationship, etc.). Set sacred intention to seek God Within and follow the flow of Spirit in your life as you undergo deaths and rebirths.

CHAPTER 34

FINDING GOD IN ALL:
1 Samuel 16:14-17:11

The reality of the events remembered on Good Friday (Jesus' trial, flogging, and crucifixion) invites questions about good and evil in our lives. The Good Friday ritual of stripping the church altar and covering it with a black cloth is redeemed on Easter Sunday with the crispness of white altar linens and fresh flowers. New life comes.

Verse 23, "And whenever a spirit from God came upon Saul, David would take his harp and play on it, so that Saul found relief; he recovered and the evil spirit left him alone."

C.G. JUNG STATES that the Self, the totality of psyche/soul, is "the author of both that which is helpful and that which is injurious to the self." The reading from 1 Samuel illustrates that God Within contains all: the evil spirit, the helper, the comforter, and our ego. The story invites us to consider our response to the evil spirit in us. Saul realizes the presence of the evil spirit and wants relief from it. He receives the comfort that also comes from God Within.

The evil spirit usually shows up in feelings and actions that are destructive to us. It prompts attitudes, actions, and responses that work against the forward movement of life. It hijacks life-giving energies and spins them into life thwarting feeling states. The evil spirit distorts. Bits of self that would naturally find their way into our integrated sense of self become larger than life and terrorize us. Catastrophic thinking and out of proportion emotional responses are two examples.

The evil spirit may manifest in compulsions, worries, discontent, overwhelming anxiety, feelings of flying apart, compulsions that result in self destructive behaviors leading to addictions, and circular patterns of self sabotage. Common examples include lifestyle patterns (such as overeating, lack of exercise) that destroy our health, staying in relationships to maintain status quo even though we are slowing losing connection to God Within, stopping a creative project that brings joy because others are critical, and cutting off interactions out of fear.

Emotionally, misapplied force (of feelings) often appears as "evil spirits." Emotions show up as messengers—information about who we are and what we need—and we often ignore, overlook, or deny them. The energy of these emotions then turn on us and create depression, confusion, unknowing, rage, paranoia, or other states that separate us from God Within or the Self.

Fritz Perls, founder of Gestalt Therapy, said, "Depression is anger turned inward." Confusion often appears to mask fear of what is known. Unknowing often is the denial of our embodied (felt sense) experience. Rage often appears after the dismissal of anger that has informed us of needed changes. Paranoia results from the lack of integration of inner experience with present reality.

Saul called upon David with his harp when he experienced an "evil spirit." We too can call on another aspect of Self to soothe and free us from being swallowed by the negative. Music often facilitates such a shift. Angeles Arrien states that there are four universal healing salves: singing, dancing, storytelling, and solitude. Moving into these activities can be our way of "calling upon David to play his harp." God Within provides a means of comfort even in the presence of an "evil spirit."

Inner Reflection

I invite you to consciously attend to whatever "evil spirit" may present by using one of the healing salves. When the "evil spirit" has left, consider the energy or emotion behind it. Ask, what is the inner experience that needs to be unblocked and allowed to flow naturally outward? What thoughts, actions, and embodied experiences effortlessly come as you do this? Be courageous, and move with the flow of your larger God Within.

CHAPTER 35

YOU ARE GOD'S TEMPLE:
1 Corinthians 2:14–3:15

We easily think of Jesus as having been an embodiment of God. We know that his death and resurrection was a symbolic tearing down of the body Temple and rebuilding it in three days. As followers of Jesus the Christ, our path is Incarnation: God becoming flesh in us. Our body mind is God's Temple.

Verse 16, "Surely you know that you are God's temple, where the Spirit of God dwells."

PAUSE AND REFLECT on the importance of the scripture, "…you are God's temple, where the Spirit of God dwells." It is within us, in our body mind, that the Spirit of God lives. We do not have to look outside of our selves for the Divine. We need only to look within ourselves. Jung wrote, "If we really knew, the body and the mind are different densities of the same energy." I believe the "same energy" Jung references is the Breath of God (*Ruach*). It is the spiritual energy that takes form even in our DNA. We refer to it as our libido or *chi* or life force.

I was recently in the company of a pathologist who had become a Jungian Analyst. He shared research that substantiates the connection between DNA removed from the body and secluded in a laboratory test tube and the person's body mind even when separated by 200 miles. The DNA responds to shifts in the person's state of consciousness (emotions and sensations) although separated from the body by great distance. The connection is the Mystery of life, the Ruach that manifests in us. It is not subject to laws of time and space. The Divine essence in the DNA removed from the body continues to respond as if it were still connected to the person physically. The scripture above invites us to remember what we knew innately at birth and what science is researching. Our body, our cellular consciousness, is where the Spirit of God lives.

We all have had experiences that separated us from knowing our body mind. Early experiences where our innate, instinctive sensibility was denied or dismissed or violated set up mistrust in our embodied experience. When we moved according to our internal promptings, we may have felt shame and guilt as our autonomy and initiative were not in sync with those around us. The tempering of our instinctive self that is a necessary part of the human experience may have squashed and stifled, rather than balanced, our nature. We end up being separated from and devaluing our body as God's temple.

We have to reclaim the presence of God Within all of our body mind. All of our sensations, intuitions, thoughts, and feelings express a bit of God Within. As we hold this truth, we can receive all that is within us as an expression of the Spirit of God. We know our selves to be God's temple.

Inner Reflection

Take a few minutes to consider your relationship to yourself as God's temple. How do you tend your body mind? How do you track the connections between your ego/conscious self and the body responses that come from the unconscious? Begin to greet each sensation, emotion, intuition, thought, and feeling as an expression of God Within. Where are distortions from the past interfering with your knowing your oneness with God? Meditate on the scripture noted above to feel your value and importance as an embodiment of God.

CHAPTER 36

TRUSTING THE CALL TO SACRIFICE:
Genesis 22:1–18

*We do not always understand the processes of transformation.
We may question and struggle against the initial stage of sacrifice
as it means something dies. Jesus struggled in the Garden of
Gethsemane, as he knew death was approaching. When we
make a sacrifice of the good for the better or the better
for the best, new life always comes.*

Verse 2, "God said, 'take your son Isaac, your only son,
whom you love, and go to the land of Moriah. There
you shall offer him as a sacrifice on one of the hills
which I will show you.'"

TODAY'S SCRIPTURE comes from one of the most disturbing stories of the Old Testament. When considered literally, the story evokes feelings of outrage and disbelief. To make useful meaning of the story, we must look to the deeper, implied or symbolic meaning. I offer the following symbolic associations and interpretations.

The Kabbalistic Tree of Life (an image of the energies of God that came into the soul of the world and soul of humanity at the time of Creation) associates Isaac with God as Divine Strength and Severity. We experience this energy in us as volition or willpower. The Tree associates Abraham with the emanation of Mercy and Compassion. On the Tree of Life,

Strength and Severity flows out of Mercy and Compassion.

Too often, we confuse willpower with harsh motivational techniques. Judgment, extreme action, one sidedness, self-blame, and harassment are not agents of willpower. True will is a felt conviction that easily moves forward into action. We experience it when connected to our God-given heart's desires and the promptings of our psyche/soul.

The Self, the organizing principle of our psyche, contains the libido/life force that is true volition. When we align with our life force, we have the energy we call willpower. We recognize this energy comes from following the desires of the larger Self versus the little self or ego.

Symbolically, Isaac represents the sense of volition or will that we feel in our body mind. It may or may not be self/ego generated or Self-given. Abraham represents a larger self that knows ego-generated will is unsustainable. How do we know if our sense of willpower is ego generated or Self- generated? **Mercy and Compassion always accompany Divine Will or Volition! If harsh judgments, condemnation, or abusive self-talk is present, ego generated will is present. If we feel compassion, self-acceptance, support, and energy, Divine Will is present.**

The story of Abraham going to sacrifice Isaac offers a picture of a movement necessary to clarify the will of God Within. Abraham is willing to follow what he experiences as God's direction. He is willing to sacrifice what he has helped create (his son). He trusts that the right sacrifice will be provided. He says to Isaac, "God will provide himself with a young beast for the sacrifice" (verse 8). Abraham moves forward as directed, willing to give up what he has created and sustained (his son). In the end, a ram is provided for the sacrifice. The ram is symbolic of passions and desires that are disconnected from the Self. What we have to sacrifice are the desires that are generated by the ego or adaptive self separated from God Within.

A sacrifice has to happen when we seek connection to God Within. We, our egos, must be willing to surrender what we think and feel in order to know the desires and longings of our soul. Our passions and our desires are conduits of our soul. Learning to discern what these mean as expressions of God Within requires a willingness to give up our ego interpretations of the inner experiences. We have to be willing to see beyond our current limited view. We have to let go of our preconceived ideas to open to new perspectives and behaviors. As Abraham followed what he thought was God's direction, he received redirection. We, too, have to be open to God Within directing us in unexpected, unanticipated ways.

Inner Reflection

Take a few minutes to reflect on where you are struggling. Does a sense of a sacrifice or letting go need to happen? Are you holding onto your ego-created and ego-sustained ways of interpreting and acting? Consider the passions and longings that are involved in the struggle. Ask the Self/God Within to show you the next steps in resolving the struggle. Be willing to know and act upon the desires of the Self/Divine Within.

CHAPTER 37

FACING HOSTILITIES:
1 Kings 5:1–6:1

As we move towards wholeness, we may encounter hostility towards our aliveness. The hostility may come from the outside world or from our inner processes. We may feel crucified by hatred, criticism, envy, fear, or verbal attacks. We have to deal with the hostilities so we do not get caught in inertia that leads to a slow death of our energy. We can learn to use the natural destructive energy in the cycle of creation to cut into the hostility and to discern what is true and what is needed for peace.

Verses 2-4, "Solomon (said), 'You know that my father David could not build a house in honor of the name of the Lord his God, because he was surrounded by armed nations until the Lord made them subject to him. But now on every side the Lord my God has given me peace...So I propose to build a house in honor of the name of the Lord my God...'"

HOW OFTEN OUR PLANS get sidetracked or usurped because of some hostile energy! A thought or emotion that cuts us, weighs us down, or blocks our joy grabs hold of us; we are off in a direction that has nothing to do with what we want. The hostility can come at us from the outside world or from our inner processes. People's nasty comments or veiled jabs can set in motion an onslaught of destructive self-talk and emotion. Either way, we have to deal with the hostility before we can move forward with our relationship to self, other, project, desire, etc...

We often ignore conflicts and hostilities because they are unpleasant and not what we want. We may feel helpless and think our only option is to act as if they do not exist. We may respond reflexively in a way to "keep the peace" even when hostility is interfering with our interaction. The conflicts keep showing up, uninvited at the worst possible times. They seem to accompany our forward movement, either attempting to sabotage growth or to steal the satisfaction and joy of living.

The inner Solomon, or Wise Man within, knows there is a right order to our growth. It may be time for us, as for David, to dialogue with the hostile energies. We have to know the inner feeling states, old beliefs, suspicious attitudes, or lack of trust that act like armed nations keeping us from acting on our soul's desires.

The author of Ecclesiastes (3:8) reminds us, "[there is] a time for war and a time for peace." We must live through the inner war or peace that is the next step in our journey. David's work was to deal with the armed nations around him and seek peace. Solomon's work was to build the house of the Lord.

Growth involves cycles of creation, equilibrium, and destruction. Equilibrium is experienced as balance and right order. It is the momentary state between creation and destruction. The next step towards equilibrium may be dealing with armed and defensive energies within us. We have to resolve our inner "wars" and hostilities before we can respond in healthy ways to other people's hostilities. We have to face opposing desires, hateful feelings, negating thoughts, limiting beliefs, life-destroying memories, etc. that block the flow of soul's energy. We can choose to use destructive energies that are present in the cycle of creation to cut into the hostility, to discern what is true, and to see what is needed for peace.

As we consciously acknowledge the inner "armed nations", we relate to all aspects of our psyche/soul—"the good, the bad, and the ugly," the wanted and the unwanted, the accepted and the unsanctioned, the loving and the hateful—with an intention for understanding and integration into our self. We do this by acknowledging, observing, listening, and dialoguing with the energy. In this way, we create a line of communication between our ego and our larger Self. We move to a place of consciously building the house or life that allows God Within to flow freely through us.

Inner Reflection

Take a few minutes to reflect on where you are experiencing hostility. What or who are the outer triggers? What are the inner processes—the attacking memories, thoughts, and emotions?

Ask God Within to give you strength and courage to face each one and to discern what you need. Be in ongoing relationship to each state (thought, feeling, sensation, etc.) until something shifts and you experience the free, life-giving flow of your soul. Take action to create the needed "house."

CHAPTER 38

WHAT ARE YOU LOOKING FOR?:
John 1:29–42

Judas gave Jesus over to the authorities for a bag of coins. We know of Judas' remorse when he realized what he had sought was not what he really wanted. Like Judas, we sometimes look for things in the wrong places. The most important seeking we can do is to know God Within.

Verse 38, "When he [Jesus] turned and saw them following him, he asked, 'What are you looking for?'"

WHAT WE SEEK is like a honing device for our energies! It steers us towards a destination of experience. Our known and unknown desires shape our attitudes, feelings, and actions. Where we are in this moment is a result of a confluence of our desires.

Sometimes, we are not consciously aware of what we are looking for. We find our selves with feelings and thoughts that are contrary to what we say we want. We act in ways that are contrary to what we desire. It is as if we rob our selves of the time, energy, and space to embody our heart's longings.

We are complex creatures. Our bodies and minds have multiple layers of longings that sometimes contradict one another. We may crave one thing while longing for its opposite. My favorite example is craving sweet desserts while longing to feel lighter in body by losing weight. Another is longing for companionship while wanting to avoid interdependency. When we find our selves not getting what we think we want, we have to look within to see what other desires are at work.

Being human means experiencing contradictions in what we want. We all have conflicting emotions, thoughts, and impulses. At any given moment, we might ask our selves, "What am I seeking? What do I want?" The first response is usually a big want, something other than the experience of the moment. We need to look deeper within to see the desire that we are pursuing in the present moment.

Present moment desires usually revolve around the basic needs of safety, love, belonging, and self-esteem. Our instinctive desire to survive physically, as well as psychologically is always at work. Feeling our self as a being, as a person, as a self-governing body, is primary in all our interactions (with our self and others). We want to feel like somebody in relationship to others. We even adopt ways of being that are not congruent with whom we are to fit in with others. When our desires to belong and survive get usurped by the outside world, we may lose any conscious sense of our soul's desire.

The esoteric Judeo-Christian path affirms the desire to know our self, to be in conscious relationship to our soul, and to seek union with the Divine in every situation as the highest pursuit. In the above scripture passage, two of John the Baptist's disciples began following Jesus after John proclaimed Jesus to be the Lamb of God, God's Chosen One. Those two disciples made a choice to seek relationship to the Christ.

I believe that we seek relationship to the Christ when we seek to know God Within. We are made in the image of God. The psychic structure we call the Self is the totality of our psyche/soul; Jung described it as a part of God that God put in us so that we will know there is a God. When we seek to know the seed of the Self within all of our felt experiences, we choose to follow the Christ.

Inner Reflection

What are you looking for? I invite you to let this question accompany you through the next few days. Open to seeing the layers of desire that are operating in any given moment. Let yourself acknowledge the instinctive desires for safety, love, belonging, and sense of self as well as the soulful desires for creativity, self-expression, and authentic relating. Seek to know God Within that is at the core of all your desires.

CHAPTER 39

FOLLOW YOUR GOD:
Deuteronomy 6:10–15

During Easter week, we see how Jesus followed the guidance of God in moving towards death while some around him followed lesser gods. The actions of the disciple who betrayed him, the follower who cut off the ear of the High Priest's servant, and Peter who denied knowing Jesus are examples of serving gods of the people. When we follow the Voice of Silence that is God Within, we live our soul's truth.

Verses 13-14, "The Lord your God you shall fear; him you shall serve, and by his name alone you shall swear. Do not follow other gods, any of the gods of the peoples who are all around you."

TODAY'S SCRIPTURE teaches that we are to follow and give allegiance only to "The Lord your God." In the historical context of the story, the Israelites were being reminded of the necessity to stay loyal to and serve only Yahweh. Yahweh is the Divine One that holds all and has the power to unite all. From the symbolic perspective of Jungian psychology, "the Lord your God" is the "Self."

The Self is the totality of psyche (soul), and the organizing principle of psyche. The Self holds all of the energies that come from within us—"the good, the bad, and the ugly". When we realize that our ego, the "little s" self, is but a fragment of the totality of who we are, we naturally fear the forces that show up as moods, affects, judgments, attitudes, etc. We can meet these forces with a healthy respect and awe, sometimes called fear in the scriptures, or we can meet these with the instinctive fear response of fight or flight. The fight or flight response usually shows up in judgmental, condemning attitudes and numbing, self-destructive behaviors. The healthy response shows up in the desire to understand, to learn about, and to make choices according to the truth of our soul.

The path of individuation (also known as salvation or enlightenment) means the ego/self follows the guidance and direction of God Within. Learning to distinguish the voice of the Self from "the gods of the peoples who are all around us" is a part of the process. There are always people, institutions, media, etc. that tell us what to value, how to believe/think, what to feel, and how to live. These "gods" can crowd out and cover up the perceptions, desires, and the knowings that begin in our heart (and show up in our gut).

We have internalized, learned beliefs that can also interfere with our hearing God Within. By paying attention to how our psychic energy is moving in these ways, we can begin to know the voice of God Within.

Inner Reflection

Take a few moments to follow your breath into your body and mind. Notice the feelings, emotions, thoughts, images, and desires that are present. Breathe deeper into your belly and invite the feelings and images that originate from God Within to show themselves to you. Set sacred intention to follow the energy and guidance of God WIthin.

CHAPTER 40

THE DIVINE IS HERE:
John 20:1–18

The Self/God Within stands behind, or within, every experience of our body, mind, and psyche/soul. We have only to look with eyes that see the seed of the Divine that has taken shape within us and around us. Like Mary Magdalene looking right at Jesus, but not seeing him, we sometimes miss the obvious presence of God in our lives.

Verses 13-14, "She answered, 'They have taken my Lord away, and I do not know where they have laid him.' With these words she turned round and saw Jesus standing there, but did not recognize him."

E ENCOUNTER the Divine every moment, yet we often do not recognize our Lord. We are created in the image of God, so our body and mind are reflections of Divine energy. We are meeting God in every breath. Each breath infuses our cellular consciousness with Divine Essence. Our body communicates this infusion of energy to us with the language of sensation and emotion. Our mind, meaning our intellect and desire nature working in tandem, informs us through image and word. The Divine becomes flesh in us.

We may not see the Divine, including our Self (God Within), in the present moment because we deem "what is" mundane, undesirable, and wrong. "What is" may not fit our description of what Divine looks like. The institutional church has historically devalued the body. The flesh was deemed problematic at best, demonic at worst. Such preconceived ideas, dismissal of our experiences, devaluing of our self, and deferring to outer authority block our ability to receive the Self's communications.

Mary Magdalene did not expect to see Jesus standing outside the tomb. Although she was looking for him, she did not see him initially. He was in a place and a form (body) she did not expect. She knew he had been crucified; she came looking for his tomb. Her expectations and previous experience interfered with her seeing Christ when she first saw him outside the tomb.

Like Mary Magdalene, we often do not see the Divine at first glance. Our beliefs and our history can be a fortress that creates tunnel vision. We all have learned patterns of response to our selves—our embodied experience of sensations, emotions, intuitions, thoughts, and feelings. We have patterns of moving in relationship to our self and others based on historical realities. These patterns are problematic because the present moment is not the historical one. Too often, we unwittingly live the past instead of the present. We are not able to see beyond the unconscious restraints of what has been.

Mary Magdalene's encounter with a risen Christ reminds us that we can move beyond our preconceived ideas and history. God Within stands behind, or within, every experience of our body mind, psyche/soul. We have only to look for the unexpected. To look with eyes that see the seed of the Divine that has taken shape within us. △

Inner Reflection

Begin looking at all within you as a cloaked seed of God Within. Look beyond your initial reactions to see the deeper essence of what is. If it is a negative feeling, idea, or fantasy, what is the seed energy? Place it in the context of the whole of you. How is God Within showing up unexpectedly? Seek to see God Within in every moment, place, and movement of your life.

The Divine is Here
All has its rightful place.
The me that is Divine is right here
All I have to do is to turn around
To see outside the tomb
Of old memories and past experiences
To roll away the blocks to this moment

The caves of hiding must be left
There is a time to walk into the open
To move from the womb of the old
To the free flowing light
Where life grows and moves again
All that is dead will be reborn

It is just a matter of time
Forgotten desires find outlets
Denied emotions inform our actions
The Self we lost returns
We must roll the stone away
Push back the blocks to our path

Follow the thread of our heart
To know the truth of what is
We see the Divine in this moment

APPENDIX
Meditation Summaries

1. What Do You Seek?:
Jeremiah 45:1–5

At Easter, we reflect on the prophecy of the temple being destroyed and rebuilt in three days. We know that this prophecy pointed to Jesus' bodily death and resurrection. The destroyed temple was the body. Our temple body is the sacred house of God and is the house where our ego, conscious sense of self, begins. Seeking to know God Within happens as we build, inhabit, and nourish our body mind.

2. The Wisdom Voice:
James 3:13–4:12

Lent is traditionally a time of self-reflection and contemplation. We willingly give something up to make space for knowing God Within. As we seek to know our selves in relationship to God, we can hear the inner Wisdom voice. Wisdom leads us to an acceptance and integration of our true nature. We give up hiding from our selves. We find the ability to be straightforward and sincere.

3. A New Inner Morality:
Jeremiah 7:1–15

At the time of Christ's crucifixion, the temple veil that kept people from the innermost Holy of Holies was torn open. Symbolically, the opening suggests a way of relating within our selves where nothing is hidden. All is seen. Mending our ways and our doings with our self is the first step in transformation. When we want something different in the outer world (relationships, environment, etc.), we must first change within our self.

4. A New Order:
2 Corinthians 5:14–18

The seasons of Lent and Easter invite us to reflect on the processes of change that include death and resurrection. As we join with the energies of the Self/God Within, something changes within us and ultimately around us. A new world emerges.

5. The Light of Desire:
Psalm 13

Easter and spring usher in the physical reality of more light. The days become longer than the nights. When we experience a resurrection of our heart's desires, we have more inner light or consciousness. The warmth of our soul flows into our body and mind and grows new life in our world.

6. Saved From Shame
Romans 10: 8-15

On the cross, one of the thieves being crucified along side Jesus recognized his Divinity. The thief acknowledged his wrongdoing and asked Jesus to remember him. Jesus said, "today you shall be with me in Paradise". We too can ask God Within to save us from the energetic death of paralysis that shame about our self brings.

7. The Gifts of Seeing and Hearing:
Colossians 1:9–14, Matthew 13:1–16

We live in a world of matter where we are easily seduced into thinking that what is concrete, literal, or fixed is the truth. Our minds become "gross"—filled with an occupation of that which is immediately obvious. The Easter story of crucifixion and resurrection remind us that reality is bigger than what appears in the rational, materialistic worldview.

8. Destruction for Life:
Isaiah 2:1–11

The celebration of Easter and the ancient rituals of spring remind us that life comes after death. The life force is freed when a form dies; new life comes. Learning how to use destructive impulses in service of life, instead of against life, is essential for our spiritual growth. Knowing what and when to destroy, and what and when to build is a gift of conscious relationship to God Within.

9. Finding God in Seeming Evil:
Job 1:1–10

From the cross, Jesus uttered, "My God, my God, why hast thou forsaken me?" We too sometimes feel abandoned by the Self. When we feel wronged by God or the Self, it serves us well to look for what and how the forces of destruction, creation, and integration are moving within us.

10. Transformation from Death:
Isaiah 6:1–8

Resurrection is the ultimate goal of death. Something dies and something new is born. The story of Jesus' death and his resurrection as the Christ offer us the truth of transformation. New life comes on the heels of destruction.

11. Our Completion:
Colossians 2:8–23

The lower nature of humanity is seen many times in the Easter story. Greed, self-preservation, lying, violence, and misguided ideas surround the betrayal and death of Jesus. We all have instinctive, reflexive reactions that harm us and others. We become more whole as we see through the automatic, "blind" responses of emotions, urges, impulses, and compulsions to the seed of the Divine Within that is seeking expression.

12. Following the Inner Divine:
Matthew 4:18–22, Romans 10:8b–18

Many times in his ministry, Jesus withdrew to be alone for prayer. He sought the knowing that comes only from hearing the still, small voice of God Within. He listened and followed even to death. As we speak our prayers, we hear what is in our heart. As we listen, we hear the deeper Voice of Silence that is God Within.

13. Laying Down Your Life:
1 Kings 5:1–6:1

Easter is the story of Jesus the man willingly laying down his life to be resurrected as the Christ. We are called to lay down our life for our friends by giving up the preconceived ideas we project onto them. By owning what is within us instead of putting it on them, we move towards the wholeness of the Christ as we integrate all aspects of God Within.

14. Action Required, Part 1:
Faith 2 Peter 1:1–11

The scriptures tell us that Jesus spent time preparing himself before he began his public ministry. He made choices along the way to stay rooted in what he knew his path to be. He exemplified the qualities of faith, virtue, knowledge, self-control, fortitude, piety, brotherly kindness, and love. We are called to cultivate these qualities within our nature. When we use our psychological functions of thinking, feeling, sensation, and intuition to develop these qualities, we are choosing to strengthen our connection to God Within/Self.

15. Action Required, Part 2:
Faith 2 Peter 1:1–11

Jesus prayed in the Garden of Gethsemane as he struggled with the knowledge of what was to happen to him. He went to the source of his faith, his own experience of God, with his unrest. Our journey towards wholeness involves many changes. As we follow our experience of God and act on our faith, we also need to return to the source, God Within, with our struggles.

16. Action Required, Part 3a:
Virtue 2 Peter 1:1–11

Jesus followed what he knew to be the will of the Divine for him. He moved forward throughout his life, even to death, with an embodied faith. As we cultivate the virtues of fortitude, temperance, and prudence, we align with the flow of the life force in us. We mediate the various energies within our body and mind so we know the natural direction our soul wants to go.

17. Action Required, Part 3b:
Virtue 2 Peter 1:1–11

In the Easter story, we see many examples of the lack of virtue. Pilate wanted to please the crowd even though he found no fault with Jesus. Peter denied knowing Jesus even though he followed him. The soldiers acted out the collective decision to kill. When we develop the virtue of prudence, we meet our intellectual, emotional, mental, and physical desires with wise discernment. We live the truth of our heart's desires and release the desires not of our heart.

18. Action Required, Part 3c: Justice, Fortitude, Temperance
2 Peter 1:1–11

We have a choice as to whether we live consciously in relationship to the Self/God Within, the totality of our psyche/soul. We can give our selves over to whatever comes, or we can decide which direction to move with our energies. We can go to sleep like the disciples did while Jesus was praying in the Garden, or we can stay awake. Staying awake means facing all that is in us. We need the virtues of justice, fortitude, and temperance.

19. Action Required, Part 4: Knowledge 2 Peter 1:1–11

When we seek knowledge of our embodied soul, we encounter God in the Self, the totality of our psyche/soul. As he was dying, one of the thieves crucified beside Jesus felt the truth of Jesus' presence. He had an embodied experience that prompted him to call out to Jesus. As we encounter God Within, our sense of separateness dies. We know our selves to be with the Divine in the present moment.

20. Action Required, Part 5: Self-Control 2 Peter 1:1–11

When we think of self-control as checking our thoughts and behaviors to see if they are a true expression of soul, we see how Jesus moved through his life with self-control. He moved out of the truth of his Self even expressing anger when he turned over the tables of the money changes in the temple. He consistently acted in sync with his heart even in his walk to death.

21. Action Required, Part 6: Fortitude 2 Peter 1:1–11

Jesus so clearly acted with courage as he willingly went with the soldiers who arrested him. Fortitude helped him stay the course. We need fortitude to face the inner as well as outer hostilities that we encounter seeking to know the larger Self/God Within.

22. Action Required, Part 7: Piety 2 Peter 1:1–11

The pious and godly seek to see, know, and experience God in all they encounter. They meet every situation, person, event, and thing as an expression of the Divine, including what they encounter in their inner world. To make meaning out of the events of Easter week, we have to seek to know God in destruction as well as creation, in death as well as resurrection.

23. Action Required, Part 8: Brotherly Kindness
2 Peter 1:1–11

As I imagine the last meal Jesus shared with his disciples, I feel the presence of brotherly kindness. All were included, even those whom Jesus knew would soon betray him. Imagine having an inner table

134

where you meet all parts of yourself with brotherly kindness. Practicing inner compassion allows us to practice compassion with others.

24. Action Required, Part 9:
Love 2 Peter 1:1–11

Jesus consistently acted with love. Even from the cross, he expressed a loving sentiment that his persecutors be forgiven for their ignorance. He felt his oneness with humanity and God. We cannot make love happen, but we can practice the art of loving.

25. Action Required, Part 10: Living Effectively
2 Peter 1:1–11

To encounter the risen Christ, Jesus' followers had to give up what they knew. They had to open to experiencing what they had never before encountered. We open to encounters with the Divine as we do the ego work of developing the qualities of faith, virtue, knowledge, self-control, fortitude, piety, brotherly kindness, and love.

26. Raised to New Life:
Mark 2: 1-12

Being raised in new life to Christ means we can access or connect to God Within where we can transcend/rise above the immediate state of our consciousness. We can set aside the ways of expressing and presenting our selves that keep us paralyzed. We can experience the promise of the resurrection and be freed to move in new ways.

27. Standing With Yourself:
Genesis 45: 1-15

The life cycle from conception to birth to death is filled with Mystery. The story of Jesus' birth, life, death, and resurrection exemplifies the necessity of being in the moment. It is in the present moment that we can know and find God. Jospeh stayed true to God Within even when his brothers sold him into slavery. He found new life in Pharoah's household.. Our ability to hold an open space, a space of unknowing, is essential in order to receive new life.

28. Eyes that See
Luke 11:27–36

Jesus had vision that went beyond the momentary, surface appearances. His eyes saw more than the physical plane. We too have that ability. Our ego and adaptive self often interfere with our knowing by holding onto what is obvious. The seasons of Lent and Easter call us to look into the darkness with the Light of consciousness.

29. Strengthened In Your Inner-Being: Ephesians 3:14–21

Our inner being is the conduit through which the Divine flows into us. Christ connects us to the Self. The great Mystery of the Easter story is to know our selves resurrected from the darkness of feeling separate from God. We are one with God. We seek to know and feel the unity in our body mind as we remember that God Within strengthens our being.

30. Eternal Life:
1 John 5:9–13

Christ, as the new Adam, focuses us on our inner reality and our oneness with God Within. Our conscious attention to living a unified relationship between our ego and God Within leads to a knowing of eternal life. We live through the cycles of birth, death, and resurrection that happen in our psyches/souls to experience the truth of the Easter story as we are given new life.

31. The Light of Life:
John 8:12–20

We have the light of life when we live in conscious relationship to God Within. Jesus said, "No follower of mine shall wander in the dark." When we connect to Christ within our nature, we see the larger Self, the totality of our psyche. We realize that new life has been growing in the dark, dying places. Just as the light of spring brings new growth, the light of consciousness brings new life to our body minds.

32. Do Not Be Afraid:
Matthew 14:22–33

Jesus cried out to God from the cross. He uttered his feelings. He spoke his embodied truth. The disciples cried out when they saw the unknown figure of Jesus coming towards them on the water. We too need to cry out to God Within with our deepest feelings.

33. Opening to Death/Change:
Mark 8:27–9:3

Form or matter (including the physical body) is not the essence of the life force. The essence of the life force is the consciousness of God Within. We get confused. We think the form (of beliefs, attitudes, habits, patterns) is what is holy. Jesus' death and resurrection remind us that the Divine is always bigger than what's known in the moment. Death is an opening for birth.

34. Finding God In All:
1 Samuel 16:14-17:11

The reality of the events remembered on Good Friday (Jesus' trial, flogging, and crucifixion) invites questions about good and evil in our lives. The Good Friday ritual of stripping the church altar and covering it with a black cloth is redeemed on Easter Sunday with the crispness of white altar linens and fresh flowers. New life comes.

35. You Are God's Temple:
1 Corinthians 2:14–3:15

We easily think of Jesus as having been an embodiment of God. We know that his death and resurrection was a symbolic tearing down of the body Temple and rebuilding it in three days. As followers of Jesus the Christ, our path is Incarnation:

God becoming flesh in us. Our body mind is God's Temple.

36. Trusting the Call to Sacrifice:
Genesis 22:1–18

We do not always understand the processes of transformation. We may question and struggle against the initial stage of sacrifice as it means something dies. Jesus struggled in the Garden of Gethsemane, as he knew death was approaching. When we make a sacrifice of the good for the better or the better for the best, new life always comes.

37. Facing Hostilities:
Genesis 22:1–18

As we move towards wholeness, we may encounter hostility towards our aliveness. The hostility may come from the outside world or from our inner processes. We may feel crucified by hatred, criticism, envy, fear, or verbal attacks. We have to deal with the hostilities so we do not get caught in inertia that leads to a slow death of our energy. We can learn to use the natural destructive energy in the cycle of creation to cut into the hostility and to discern what is true and what is needed for peace.

38. What Are You Looking For?:
John 1:29–42

Judas gave Jesus over to the authorities for a bag of coins. We know of Judas' remorse when he realized what he had sought was not what he really wanted.

Like Judas, we sometimes look for things in the wrong places. The most important seeking we can do is to know God Within.

39. Follow Your God:
Deuteronomy 6:10–15

During Easter week, we see how Jesus followed the guidance of God in moving towards death while some around him followed lesser gods. The actions of the disciple who betrayed him, the follower who cut off the ear of the High Priest's servant, and Peter who denied knowing Jesus are examples of serving gods of the people. When we follow the Voice of Silence that is God Within, we live our soul's truth.

40. The Divine Is Here:
John 20:1–18

The Self/God Within stands behind, or within, every experience of our body, mind, and psyche/soul. We have only to look with eyes that see the seed of the Divine that has taken shape within us and around us. Like Mary Magdalene looking right at Jesus, but not seeing him, we sometimes miss the obvious presence of God in our lives.

137

GLOSSARY
With Applied Meanings

Archetype: a *priori* structural forms in which things are conceived and perceived;
- "As an attribute of instinct, (archetypes) partake of its dynamic nature, and consequently possess a specific energy which causes or compels definite modes of behavior or impulses; that is they may have…a possessive or obsessive force." (Jung, MDR, p. 347)
- "Virtual images"; un-solid until encounter with empirical facts; must be understood with historical parallels like mythological motifs
- Inherited thought patterns
- We experience them in our body as affects.

Affect: a feeling state characterized by body sensations

Body mind: the totality of our physical, emotional, mental, and spiritual bodies working together

Chi: life force; the energy of life that flows through our body enlivening us

Complex: autonomous grouping of psychic contents characterized by a specific feeling tone, something usually hidden from sight, that includes somatic (body) innervations
- Consists of a core affect or archetype that gathers related experiences;
- It assimilates what suits it and inhibits everything else
- It is the building blocks of psyche

- Its independence in psyche stems from its affect
- It is a collection of imaginings relatively free of central control of consciousness, may bend or cross one's intentions.
- "Architect of dreams and of symptoms" (Jung, CW Vol. 8, par. 383)

Conscious: that which is known, connected to ego and sense of self

Collective Unconscious: all psychic contents that belong not to one individual, but to many
- Psychic expression of the identity of brain structure of human being and the sympathetic nervous system
- Includes latent predispositions toward identical reactions
- Mythological
- Storehouse of relics and memories of past
- Archetypes
- "In the deepest reaches, there is a layer (collective unconscious) where man is not a distinct individuality. His mind widens out and merges with mind of mankind. Mind has its basic conformity as the body does. On this level, we're all one—wholeness that cannot be dissected. This is called participation mystique." (Jung, CW Vol. 18, par. 87)

Compensation: balancing, adjusting, supplementing; completing the whole, like yin and yang

Differentiation: development of differences, separating parts from a whole

Discernment: clarity; teasing out parts from a whole to see clearly nuances of energies (i.e., separating fear from anger, hurt from rage)

Ego: center of consciousness; one's sense of self

Ego-Self axis: a term coined by Erich Neumann to describe the conscious flow of energy between the ego self and the larger, totality of Self

Enlightenment: attaining Wisdom; a state of spiritual knowledge that frees one from (from the cycles of rebirth in Buddhism)

Esoteric: secret, reserved for initiates of a tradition or system of knowledge

Feeling tone: affective state accompanied by somatic innervations including body sensations

Felt sense: a bodily felt, implicitly rich "sense of some situation, problem, or aspect of one's life; the holistic, implicit, bodily sense of a complex situation" (Gendlin, 1996, pp. 20, 58)

Focusing: Eugene Gendlin's technique for developing awareness of the processes of experiencing in our body

Gestalt Therapy: a form of psychotherapy developed by Fritz and Laura Perls; it emphasizes the experience of the body in the moment and the dialogue between the therapist and the client; it focuses on being with the client versus moving the client

Glyph: a symbolic image

Individuation: process whereby the individual personality specific to a person is developed as they differentiate from the collective

Injunction: command, strong direction

Instinct: innate automatic, reflexive responses; live in the body; Jung identifies the following five instincts: Hunger, Sexuality, Activity, Reflection, and Creativity

Kabbalah: a collection of mystical, spiritual teachings rooted in Judaism. One of the primary teachings is The Tree of Life, a relational glyph of the energies of God that came into the soul at the time of creation.

Mandala: a symbol representing the Self; typically drawn as a circle filled with colors and shapes expressing one's inner state of wholeness

Persona: mediator between ego and collective consciousness; can manifest in roles we play in relationship to the world

Personal Unconscious: Includes psychic material below threshold of consciousness, subliminal perceptions (sense perceptions not strong enough to reach consciousness), unconscious fantasies that normally compensate conscious attitude; contents are from personal experience; problematic complexes live here; also, figure of shadow often met in dreams

Salvation: being saved or protected from harm; in religion, being saved from the dire consequences of sin

Self (with capital S): totality of psyche/soul; God Within; organizing principle of psyche

self (with little s): ego; sense of who we are accompanied by powerful and ever present feeling tone of our body

Self-actualization: Abraham Maslow's term for becoming all that we are, realizing our full potential

Shadow: "negative" side of personality, sum of unpleasant qualities we like to hide and insufficiently developed functions and contents of personal unconscious

Spiritual Eye or Third Eye: the inner spiritual sense whereby we see energies that move in the invisible magnetic field around each living being

The Tree of Life: a glyph of the energies of God that came into the soul at the time of Creation; the glyph shows the interrelationship of continuous flow of the emanations of God (see diagram on page 91)

Transcendent Function: an innate, organic process whereby our psyche produces a uniting third to reconcile two opposite states of feeling, desires, etc.

Transcendent: rising above the limits of natural humanity; beyond categories of experience in the physical world

Transformation: the process from which something changes from one form into another; metamorphosis, i.e., the chrysalis turning into a butterfly, the tadpole becoming a frog

Unconscious: that which is unknown; includes ego-Self axis, the personal unconscious and the collective unconscious

Wisdom: the beginning of the knowledge of God that comes through general principles or natural laws; on The Tree of Life, the second emanation of God into the soul known in Hebrew as Chokmah

ANNOTATED BIBLIOGRAPHY

Adler, G., Fordham, M., McGuire, W., Read, H. (Eds.) (1969) *The Collected Works of C. G. Jung.* Princeton: Princeton University Press.
The Collected Works of C. G. Jung are an endless resource for understanding psyche/soul in all its manifestations.

Arrien, Angeles (1993). *The Four-Fold Way: Walking the Paths of the Warrior, Teacher, Healer, and Visionary.* San Francisco: HarperSanFrancisco.
Arrien shares the wisdom of indigenous cultures in walking the paths of the archetypal warrior, teacher, healer, and visionary to live in balance with our inner nature and the natural world. She explores the following principles: Show Up 100%, Pay attention to what has Heart and Meaning, Telling the truth without blame or judgment, Be open to outcome (not be attached).

Fortune, Dion (1984). *The Mystical Qabalah.* York Beach: Samuel Weiser, Inc.
Fortune presents a thorough explanation of the Tree of Life as studied in the Western Mystery Tradition. This is a book for study, not easy reading.

Fromm, Eric. (1956). *The Art of Loving.* New York: Harper & Brothers Publisher.
Fromm states in the forward, "(This book) wants to convince the reader that all his attempts for love are bound to fail, unless he tries most actively to develop his total personality, so as to achieve a productive orientation; that satisfaction in individual love cannot be attained without the capacity to love one's neighbor with true humility, courage, faith, and discipline." (p. xix)

Gendlin, E. T. (1996). *Focusing-oriented psychotherapy.* New York: Guilford.
Gendlin addresses the use of focusing in various psychotherapeutic modalities.

_____ (1981). *Focusing.* New York: Bantam.
The go to book for learning the technique of focusing. It breaks focusing down into 6 steps: clearing a space, felt sense, handle, resonating, asking, and receiving

Hardon, Fr. S. J. *Meaning of Virtue in Thomas Aquinas.* https://www.ewtn.com/library/SPIRIT/MEANVIR.TXT.
Hardon summarizes Thomas Aquinas' teachings on virtue.

Jung, C. G. (1989). *Memories, Dreams, and Reflections.* New York: Vintage Books.
Jung's autobiography deals with the inner happenings of Jung himself. He shares the personal inner experiences out of which his theories grew.

Maslow, Abraham (1968) *Toward a Psychology of Being.* New York: John Wiley & Sons.
Maslow is the father of humanistic psychology. He believed our inner nature is "intrinsically neutral or positively good". His theories of self-actualization and the hierarchy of needs are pivotal in understanding our development as human beings.

Weatherhead, Leslie (1972). *The Will of God.* Nashville: Abingdon Press.
Weatherhead talks about the intentional, circumstantial, and ultimate will of God. A series of sermons he wrote during WWII in response to people saying the death of young soldiers must be God's will.

ABOUT THE AUTHOR

KATHLEEN WILEY

Kathleen Wiley is a is a Diplomate in Analytical Psychology. She is licensed as a Marriage and Family Therapist and a Professional Counselor and has a private practice in Davidson, North Carolina. Her background includes a B.A. in Christian Education and a Masters in Human Development and Learning. Her work focuses on empowering people to live out of a conscious relationship to the Self/God Within. She realizes the importance of encountering God as part of the human experience of being in a physical body and the importance of interpersonal experiences of relationship.

She is the author of this book, *NEW LIFE: Symbolic Meditations on the Promise of Easter and Spring* which offers meditations for the Easter season and *NEW LIFE: Symbolic Meditations on the Birth of the Christ Within*, offering meditations on the season of Lent.

About the Cover Photo

Kathleen took the cover photo on her honeymoon, inspired by the opening created by the greenery as she walked towards the beach on Seabrook Island. As she was taking pictures, she saw something zoom across the walkway and later saw a black and orange winged creature in her photo.

Our encounters with the Inner Divine Spirit sometimes happen like this. They come out of nowhere when our focus is on something else, and we do not know what we experienced until later. The photo seemed like the perfect opening to NEW LIFE.

About Butterfly Symbology

Cross-culturally, the butterfly is a symbol of transformation. In the Christian tradition, the butterfly symbolizes resurrection (the ultimate transformation from death to new life). The butterfly is also considered as a symbol of the soul. Our transformation leads to our ego/self becoming a beautiful, animated expression of our soul. The caterpillar disappears into the cocoon and emerges totally changed into a beautiful, winged being.

The symbolic lesson of the butterfly is the ongoing acceptance of changes in our lives. We let go of the old forms, sense of self, ways of being (the caterpillar) to emerge into the new life giving, enlivening ways of being and moving (the butterfly). Change ensures growth. The butterfly reminds us that we go through multiple stages in our life as we grow into our soul's fullness.

Yellow butterflies represent new life and prosperity in many cultures. Blue butterflies represent joy, happiness, love, and beauty. Black butterflies, sometimes used as a symbol of death, are associated with change, transition, freedom and rebirth. White butterflies signify good luck and a good life. The monarch butterfly reminds us that every moment of life is valuable; it invites us to find joy and thankfulness no matter what our situation. The luna moth symbolizes change and calls us to live for what our souls love.

The darting flight of the butterfly represents the mind and our ability to change it when necessary. The Greek word for butterfly also means *psyche*. Whenever we encounter a butterfly, we are invited to connect with our psyche/ soul.

About Flower Symbology

The butterflies are shown among two wild spring flowers, the violet and the strawberry.

Few flowers have symbolized the renewal of spring as much as the violet. As the violet hides its flowers within heart shaped leaves, it's been called the "Flower of Modesty." The pure white blooms of the wild strawberry have many positive attributes, notably righteousness and spiritual merit.

Both flowers represent the Trinity. The Monks of the Middle Ages referred to the violet as the "Herb of the Trinity" and the strawberry's trifoliate leaf structure is also symbolic of the Trinity.

The hearty strawberry bears sweet fruit, fulfilling the promise of spring.